JAMEST

AND THE

FOUNDING OF THE NATION

Warren M. Billings

Contents

Prologue

Jamestown.

The word evokes a place familiar to twentieth-century Americans as one of the most hallowed historic sites in the United States. Their nation began at this spot.

In the spring of 1607, a band of one hundred and four men and boys planted an English toehold in the New World. For the next nine decades Jamestown was the hub of England's oldest American dominion. What happened there in those years had profound significance not only for Virginia but for the subsequent history of the United States as well.

John Rolfe's experiments with tobacco laid the foundations for the colony's economic development, and they helped to expand England's commerce. They also contributed to the emergence of the British colonial system, just as Rolfe served as the prototype for a distinctly American species of entrepreneur — someone who combined discrete, seemingly disparate bits of information into profitable uses.

Promoters touted Virginia as a land of promise, and their blandishments struck receptive ears. Expectations of gaining a tract of land, a fortune, or a better life enticed colonists to exchange a familiar world for the uncertainties of North America. Whatever their reasons for emigrating, their leaving England prompted one of the greatest human migrations of all time. From the seventeenth to the twentieth century, more than sixty million Europeans, Africans, and Asians left their homelands to settle in what became the United States.

High hopes and unyielding determination were no warrants for automatic success; if anything, the odds always favored failure. The original backers of the Jamestown venture bankrupted themselves while tens of thousands of would-be settlers suffered privations, disease, and death without ever having realized their dreams. Those who survived to attain their goals interpreted their successes as a sign of divine grace, and from that belief arose the idea that Americans were a people apart, called by divine providence to special purposes.

Loose ties between Jamestown and London afforded some Virginia colonists freedom to experiment with the forms of government and the mysteries of power. They were at liberty to tailor their understanding of the mother country's law and politics to their particular interests. The General Assembly, the county courts, and the parish vestries established vital precedents for the evolution of a political system that guarantees in Thomas Jefferson's immortal phrase "life, liberty, and the pursuit of happiness."

For some Virginians, freedom meant deprivation; for others it meant bondage. The Indians whose succor spared Jamestown more than once had cause to regret their generosity; their ways clashed with English

5

ways, and they became embroiled in a losing struggle to maintain their cultural identity. That contest fixed the tragic pattern that governed Indian-white relations for three centuries. Indentured servants and slaves were valued more for their labor than their humanity. Their presence helped form American attitudes toward peoples of other races and colors. It also raised the issue of the place of dependent populations in relation to a larger society, which is a question that still requires an answer.

To visit Jamestown today is to find but small reminders of these beginnings. It little resembles what the colonists first saw or later built. Unlike Plymouth, Massachusetts, there is no longer even a town. A stark ruin — the tower of the 1639 brick church — is Jamestown's only standing seventeenth-century structure. Except for what has been recovered through archaeological fieldwork, the other physical remains have either washed into the relentless, brown waters of the James, or they still lie buried about the island. Records that could give the historian a detailed view of the place are also mostly gone, lost to fire, war, and carelessness.

Recounting the story of the tiny town on the James is a difficult, but not an impossible undertaking. Its retelling is worth the effort. Long ago, Richard Eden, an early champion of English expansion into the New World, explained why.

> The minde of man is nurysshed with knowleage, and taketh pleasure in divisinge or excogitatinge sume honest thinge, whereby it not onely leaveth among men a memorie of his immortall nature, but also engendereth the like affection in others that delite to see and heare such things as are commendable in their predicesours.[1]

A Note On Style And Documentation

In the quotations from original manuscripts and documents that appear throughout this book, the following style is observed. Dates are Old Style. That is, they are according to the ancient Julian calender, which Continental Europeans abandoned in 1582 when they replaced it with one devised by Pope Gregory XIII. That change required advancing dates by ten days; thus October 5, 1582 became October 15. The English, however, continued to use the Old Style until 1752. They also began the year on 25 March, and it was therefore customary for them to write both years, i.e., January 1, 1600/01, in the interval between January 1 and March 24, 1601. That usage is retained here, although 1 January is taken as the start of a given year.

The texts are regularized only to the extent that modern orthography is imposed on proper names, archaic abbreviations or symbols are rendered in full, and sentences begin with capitals and end in periods, question marks, or exclamation points. Use of *i*, *j*, *u*, and *w* also conforms to modern practice.

Chapter 1

England's Route to Jamestown

It was a cold December day. A damp sea breeze bore skirling gulls aloft as it carried the sounds and smells of London's bustling port across the Thames. Along one of the docks, longshoremen and sailors hurried as they loaded the last bit of cargo aboard the *Susan Constant,* the *Godspeed,* and the *Discovery.* The ships' masters urged even greater haste, lest they miss the tide and add to the delay of starting their voyage. Below decks, passengers, who had boarded the night before, moved about the cramped space in search of comfortable spots to lodge for the duration of their journey. Tight quarters and fouling air made some of the landlubbers wonder if they and sea travel were meant for each other. Battened hatches signaled that the loading was finally finished. Just as the tide ebbed, the skippers bawled out orders to cast off. Seamen ran quickly to their stations, some to climb the rigging so they could shake loose the sails, others to man the halyards, braces, or moorings. Sails fell from their lashings as the bow and spring lines were slipped. Each helmsman deftly steered his drifting vessel to catch the momentum of the wind and the running tide. Gathering speed, the tiny convoy dropped down the Thames toward the sea.

There was little in this scene to attract anyone's notice. Such sailings were everyday occurrences in the life of England's largest and busiest seaport. If someone who worked the London docks *had* paused to watch those three small ships pass that particular day in late 1606, he might have thought that they merely bespoke the importance of trade for his country. But the passengers, crew, and backers alike knew that this voyage was no ordinary commercial enterprise. For them it signified a revival of English efforts to colonize in the New World.

More than a century had passed since Christopher Columbus first anchored in the West Indies and spurred the great age of discovery of new lands in America, Asia, and Africa. The advantage of early discovery lay with the Spanish, whose conquistadors captured an empire fabled for its land, treasure, and subject peoples. Nevertheless, Columbus's exploits caught the fancy of King Henry VII, who, in 1497, sent John and Sebastian Cabot across the Atlantic to claim a portion of North America for England. West Country fishermen followed the Cabots and worked the rich North American fisheries. They often put in along the cold, forbidding Newfoundland coast to cure their catches. Sometimes, they even settled temporarily, but few other Englishmen saw in these activities a basis for colonizing the New World, despite the proddings of early promoters like Richard Eden, John Frampton, and Thomas Nicholas.

By the sixteenth century trade had increased, expanding first into traditional markets and then into places opened by the new discoveries. Improvements in farming methods enabled landowners to be more aggressive in the commercial exploitation of their holdings. Commercialized agriculture drove thousands of Englishmen from the land. They joined the ranks of a vagrant population swelled by rising birth rates and an economy that could not expand swiftly enough to accommodate their needs. Their growing numbers contributed to a sense that overcrowding threatened order throughout the realm. Order and rank, obedience and authority — these were the values of a society that divided itself not into classes, as is now the custom among Western nations, but between the rulers and the ruled. One's standing was fixed by the accident of birth, which placed an individual somewhere along a complex hierarchy of ranks that only the monarch or luck might change, and in the fluid world of sixteenth-century England, such alterations in rank were common occurrences.

For all of the changes, sixteenth-century Englishmen did not see before them years of unending expansion or matchless opportunity. Many of them believed they lived in grim, desperate times in which depression and war threatened their national existence. They hungered for adventure and achievement as explorers' tales whetted their appetites for discovering new worlds of their own. Someday England would take its rightful place among Europe's imperial powers. The beginnings of that day came toward the latter half of Queen Elizabeth I's long reign.

A woman of ready wit and consummate political skill, Elizabeth used her endowments to keep her realm safe from civil war or frequent foreign entanglements, and in doing that, she gave her subjects the chance to turn their creative talents toward founding an American empire. The Hakluyt cousins, Richard the Elder and Richard the Younger, provided the inspiration for such an undertaking. They envisioned the possession of American colonies as England's undoubted right. Moreover, they conceived of these colonies as essential to the nation's future economic development; such settlements could obviously furnish needed raw materials, additional markets, and places to employ England's surplus population. Honor, glory, *and* profit would surely accrue to those of their countrymen who took up the cause of overseas expansion. Their emphasis on these possibilities, in addition to their persistence as colonial publicists, helped to determine English thinking about America; their unflagging devotion to an idea kept it alive in times when their countrymen's vision of empire faded.

Courtiers, not merchants, were the first Elizabethans to test the Hakluyts' theories. First came Martin Frobisher, who, in 1576, tried to colonize Baffin Island as a way station in his quest for the Northwest

Passage. Next, it was the turn of Sir Humphrey Gilbert, who hoped that by settling on the Newfoundland coast he would succeed where Frobisher had failed. He did not. Then came Gilbert's half brother, Sir Walter Ralegh.* Ralegh benefited from the earlier failures; moreover, he had his Irish colonizing experiences and a larger fortune on which to draw, but his luck was no better than that of Frobisher or Gilbert. Three times he tried to erect a settlement at Roanoke Island, on the North Carolina coast, and each time his efforts were unsuccessful. The outbreak of the Anglo-Spanish War in 1588 put a stop to colonizing, as well as any attempt to resupply the fabled "Lost Colony," whereupon Ralegh lost his taste for further ventures.

For as long as the Spanish War continued, few Englishmen thought much on the value of a colonial empire in the New World, and so the idea waned. What little flicker of life remained to it was kept alive by the younger Hakluyt, who continued to publicize it at every chance that came his way. The opening of a new century, the death of Elizabeth, and the prospect of peace were encouraging signs to Hakluyt, as were modest

Sir Walter Ralegh

---

* The more familiar spelling *Raleigh* was one that Ralegh never used himself. Throughout all of his adult life, he preferred the spelling *Ralegh*, and that is why it is used here.

King James I

efforts at exploring the New England and Virginia coasts. More importantly, Hakluyt finally convinced the merchants that England stood to gain from American settlements even if they failed to yield gold or passages to the Orient. When peace returned in 1604, the merchants had already come to perceive the founding of colonies as an integral element in the progress of trade and investment opportunities.

A short while later, Hakluyt and his soldier friends Sir Thomas Gates and Edward Maria Wingfield; as well as Sir Thomas Smythe, a prominent member of the East India Company; Sir John Popham, the Lord Chief Justice of England, and other influential public men or merchants from London, Bristol, and Plymouth, started planning a new colony. They prepared the draft of a charter of incorporation and a land grant; then they petitioned King James I for permission to attempt the settlement. More than a year of lobbying passed before the king issued the appropriate letters patent on April 10, 1606.

James's charter parceled North America in half. It gave the northern part to the patentees from Bristol and Plymouth, while the remainder of the continent went to the Londoners. It required each group to organize separate privately funded and managed joint-stock companies, centered in Plymouth and London, each of whom answered to a council appointed by King James. For his part, the king promised that the colonists and their descendants "shall have and enjoy all liberties Franchises and Immunities within anie our dominions . . . as if they had been abiding and borne within this our Realme of England."[1] The charter also gave requirements for converting the natives and detailed instructions on how settlement should be accomplished, as well as the provision of resident councils to provide local government. Subsequently, the patentees prepared amplifying instructions to delineate the duties of the resident councils or to provide other advice. One of these required that "for the good Government of the people to be planted in those parts and for the good ordering and disposing of all causes happening within the same, the same to be done for the substance thereof, as neer to the Common Lawes of England, and the equity thereof, as may be."[2]

While that statement, together with the charter's warrant of individual

Sir Thomas Gates

13

Sir Thomas Smythe

rights, seemed to indicate an intent to transfer a full measure of English society to America, it was not. What concerned the patentees was not founding an England in miniature but assuring a sound, efficient business organization. Both provisions were therefore intended to aid the resident officials and to lengthen the odds of success; no one in 1606 could have anticipated the colonists' later use of these guarantees.

It was just such thinking that led the patentees to turn to the joint-stock company as their model of organization and management. The merchants among them had long employed the device to pool capital, knowledge, and talent in developing trade to eastern Europe and the Orient. Apart from its advantage to the merchants, the joint-stock company also afforded someone with no money the chance to risk his labor as a servant against a share of the anticipated profits. Here then was a means of recruiting colonists from the ranks of the poorer sorts of Englishmen.

Seven Londoners organzied themselves as the Virginia Company of London. Sir Henry Montague and Sir William Wade were influential lawyers, while Sir Walter Cope and Sir George Moore had close political ties to the court. Sir William Romney, like his colleague, Sir Thomas Smythe, was a prominent figure in the East India Company. The seventh investor, John Eldred, was an ex-privateer turned merchant who also had links with the East India Company. Their ideas for what kind of colony they should erect were shaped by the second Ralegh expedition. That is, they conceived their initial undertaking as an exploratory venture whose members would scout out a site and begin a suitable settlement on which later colonists would build a permanent colony.

Mounting the expedition took months, as the company's officials purposefully set about hiring vessels, stockpiling supplies, recruiting prospective colonists, and selecting trustworthy men for the resident council. Smythe and his colleagues had no difficulty marshaling the supplies or chartering three vessels. Two of them, the *Susan Constant* and the *Godspeed*, were chosen for their cargo capacity, while the third, the smaller pinnace the *Discovery*, was selected for her maneuverability in coastal waters.

The leaders of the expedition were an odd assortment of individuals, as were those chosen for colonists. Edward Maria Wingfield, one of the suitors for the charter, was an experienced soldier of genteel origins. George Kendall, a man of ungovernable temperament, was a spy for King James's principal minister, Robert Cecil, the Earl of Salisbury. A third councilor was John Smith, a Lincolnshire farm boy with keen instincts for survival and command that he had honed with years of soldiering on the continent. The remaining four were mariners. Of these, John Martin and John Ratcliffe lacked reputation or connection. By contrast, Christopher Newport and Bartholomew Gosnold were close to Smythe, Romney, and Eldred, and both men were familiar with the Virginia coast. Newport was given command of the expedition until it reached its destination. Company officials recruited about 105 men and boys for colonists. Half were laborers, artisans, or craftsmen; the remaineder were gentlemen unused to work of any sort.

Spring gave way to summer and summer to fall before the ships began to take on their cargoes. By the third week of November 1606 the backers drafted the last of their instructions and saw to final details. Everything seemed in readiness, but as her crew moved the *Susan Constant* "over against Ratcliff Crosse," she collided with another vessel.[3] She sustained no great damage, though the collison delayed the departure. For the moment, the words of Michael Drayton's exhortation,

> Britons, you stay too long,
> Quickly aboard bestow you,
> And with a merry gale,
> Swell your stretch'd sail, With vows as strong
> As the winds that blow you . . .[4]

seemed more a taunt than an encouragement. The disappointment was momentary; the carpenters completed their repairs toward the end of December, and on the 20th, the convoy set sail.

Once the ships cleared the Thames estuary, a contrary wind held them in sight of England for more than six weeks. It finally shifted and drove the convoy south to the Canary Islands, where the colonists stopped for fresh water and a brief respite from shipboard life. Admiral Newport then pointed his fleet on a westerly course for the West Indies. The adventurers arrived off Martinique in March 1607, and they spent a restful three weeks in the islands before sailing north toward the Virginia Capes. They were overtaken on this leg of the voyage by a "vehement tempest, which lasted all the night with winds, raine, and thunders, in a terrible manner" that drove them far from their intended course.[5] Newport did not regain his bearings for several days, but on "the sixth and twentieth day of Aprill, at foure a clocke in the morning" the English "descried the land of Virginia" and "entred the Bay of Chesupioc [i.e., Chesapeake]."[6]

Working cautiously past the great bay's headlands, Newport maneuvered his fleet farther up the bay as he searched the shore for a likely anchorage. He sighted a spot close to the south shore some eight miles west of its mouth. Quickly, he gave the order to douse sail and drop anchor. No sooner had the ships come to rest than the admiral took a

In late April 1607, the colonists first sighted the coast of Virginia. At Cape Henry, named for the Prince of Wales, they erected a cross and thanked God for their safe passage.

16

The Susan Constant, the God Speed, and the Discovery off Jamestown Island.

landing party ashore. The explorers spent the remainder of the day scouting the countryside before turning back to the place where they had left the longboat. Their retreat was temporarily blocked by some Indians who attacked with what George Percy described as "a great noise." A brief skirmish ensued, though the natives retired as soon as they had spent their arrows. Aside from a few injuries, all of Newport's men returned safely to the fleet, a bit shaken for the experience.[7]

The next morning, the ship's carpenters assembled a dismantled shallop that the colonists had brought with them. She was a sloop-rigged craft that was larger than a longboat, but smaller than the *Discovery*. Her size made her ideal for exploring coastal or inland waters. As soon as she was fitted up, the colonists started to scout the bay. First, they explored the south shore. Then, they landed at both capes, naming the southern one for Henry, Prince of Wales, and the northern one for the prince's younger brother, Charles. They also discovered that the site of their initial anchorage was actually in the mouth of a large river which they called James in honor of their sovereign. Sailing across to the James's north bank, they came to what is now called Old Point Comfort, where they found the native village of Kecoughtan. The inhabitants received them cordially, and they stayed at Kecoughtan several days before Newport pushed the fleet higher up the James. He found his next anchorage some forty miles above Old Point Comfort, off another Indian village, Paspahegh. Again, the natives treated Newport and the others kindly, so they tarried there while a party led by George Percy took the shallop to investigate farther upriver. Percy rejoined the fleet at Paspahegh on May 12, with the news that he had located a place, soon to be named "Archer's Hope," that was suitable for the main settlement. Game, fresh water, and trees abounded, and there was a good anchorage. Newport, Wingfield, and the other leaders chose to ignore Percy's site. Instead, they picked a location beyond Archer's Hope that seemed nearer to sound military thinking and the company's instructions. On the morning of May 13, the fleet anchored off a peninsula that ran out from the north bank of the James. They called the place Jamestown.

The James River provided a deep mooring for the ships at the shore of Jamestown Island.

Chapter 2
This New Land, Virginia

What the colonists called Jamestown was a pear-shaped peninsula approximately two miles long and about a mile wide. A narrow isthmus connected the western end to the north bank of the James, and as the island was almost surrounded by water, it appeared easy to defend against the Indians. Moreover, the site lay about sixty miles inland from the coast, which also made it safe from possible Spanish assaults. Game and trees appeared to be abundant, while the proximity of deep water to the shoreline meant that the mariners could moor the *Susan Constant*, the *God Speed*, and the *Discovery* to trees and unload their cargoes without the need of using the longboats to transfer the supplies ashore.

Nevertheless, there were drawbacks that were not immediately evident. First, most of the island was marsh, and that watery terrain bred enormous swarms of mosquitoes. The high ground there either rimmed the shoreline or ran out into the marsh. Second, the island lacked any

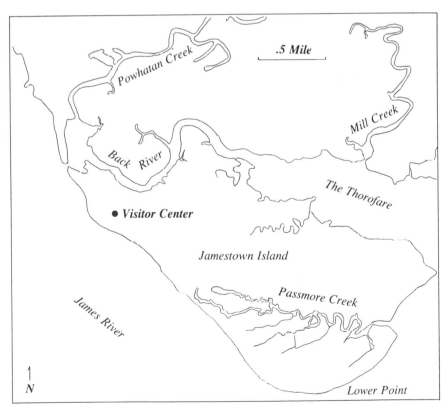

Jamestown Island

fresh water springs for drinking. The water in the marsh and the James was brackish, that is, partly salt. Finally, Jamestown was the land of a nearby tribe of Indians, the Paspaheghs, who were hardly thrilled to see strangers seated on it. Unfortunately, none of these liabilities was apparent to unskilled pioneers who chose the location for the first settlement.

Their ignorance in these matters is understandable because Jamestown's first settlers arrived at their destination with little accurate knowledge of the world they intended to inhabit. There were neither maps of the Chesapeake Bay and its tributary rivers nor detailed descriptions of the land and its natural attributes. What the English believed about Virginia arose wholly from stories promoters and earlier explorers told of the place. These accounts likened it to a paradise inhabited by simple, friendly people who were sometimes cunning and dangerous, but always savage. The eager colonists landed expecting to subdue this land of plenty and its natives to their dominion and to profit handsomely from its uses.

Paradise Virginia was not, although its endowments were beautiful and plenteous beyond any Englishman's imagination. Its climate, its soil, and its terrain changed as the land rose from the flat seacoast to the interior mountains, while its native inhabitants were hardly the simple savages the English conceived them to be. These and other physical qualities soon captured the colonists' fancies, which led to an unending speculation that gave rise to the many accounts from which come all modern portraits of primeval Virginia.

Colonial Virginia contained a territory greatly larger than the modern commonwealth. Initially, King James I's charter of 1606 defined the boundaries as everything that lay between the Passamaquoddy Bay in Maine and the Cape Fear River in North Carolina extending westward to the Pacific Ocean. By the 1660s, the founding of colonies in New England, Maryland, and the Carolinas pared down the northern and southern limits nearly to those of today, but the western border continued unfixed. Within those bounds colonial Virginia comprised four distinct topographical regions that ranged from the Atlantic coastal plain to the interior of the continent.

The Tidewater was the first of these regions. Tidewater encompassed all of Virginia between the Atlantic Ocean and the fall line, the point approximately one hundred miles inland at which the eastern rivers were no longer tidal; hence the name Tidewater. Tidewater's most obvious feature was the Chesapeake Bay, encircled by the western mainland and a large eastern peninsula that the English called the "Eastern Shore." Numerous creeks and small rivers flowed into the great bay, as did four

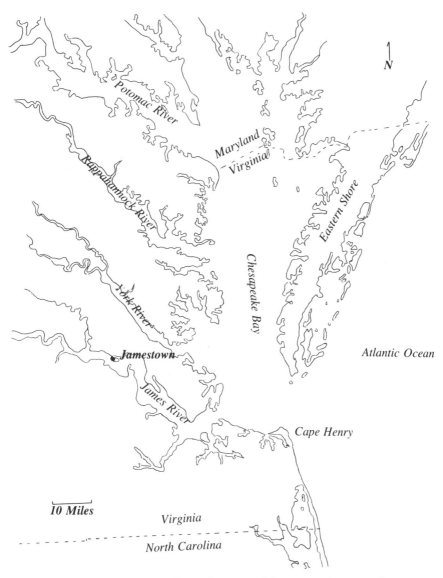

Jamestown in relationship to the coasts of the present-day states of Maryland, North Carolina and Virginia.

major tributaries — the James, the York, the Rappahannock, and the Potomac — which were themselves fed by lesser waterways. Lying beyond Tidewater were the Piedmont, the Great Valley of Virginia, the Appalachian Mountains, and the trans-Appalachian West, but colonial knowledge of these regions was sparse before 1700. The difficulty of overland travel above the fall line, fear of the Indians, and the reliance

21

on the sea link to England kept most of the English in the Tidewater until well into the eighteenth century.

Tidewater had a moderate climate, though it differed from anything in the colonists' experience. Spring came in the middle of March, and the danger of frost passed within six weeks of its coming. The mild days of spring warmed into the muggy days of July and August which were the hottest and most oppressive of the year. "Sometimes," the historian Robert Beverley noted, "very loud and surprizing Thunder" broke the heat with rain that lasted "but a few Hours at a time, and sometimes not above half an Hour, and then immediately [succeeded] clear sunshine."[1] Summer's sultriness abated toward the end of September, and the October frosts ushered in fall, that most beautiful of all Tidewater's seasons. Then came winter, which Beverley described as "very short," though frequently punctuated with "very hard Frosts."[2] Temperatures ranged from below 0° to 100°, but the averages were somewhat less extreme. Rain amounted to about 40 inches yearly, with the greatest amounts falling between April and September. It snowed in December, January, and February. More common than snow was a sharp drizzle that magnified winter's cold dreariness. Generally, however, the colonists came to regard the climate as lying "between the extreams of Heat and Cold, but inclining to the first."[3]

The Rev. John Clayton pronounced Tidewater land "a very fertile Soil, far surpassing *England*."[4] It was certainly that, though few Englishmen of the Jamestown era appreciated the delicacy of the soil's fertility. An alluvial soil called loam covered the Tidewater lowlands. Various organic compounds enriched it, but its light texture meant that it eroded easily. Without fallowing or fertilizing, it lost its productive capacity; indeed, as of 1700, erosion and loss of fertility were already serious problems for some Tidewater planters.

At the time of the colonists' first landing, and for more than a century thereafter, Tidewater sustained a world of plant and animal life whose immense variety is now difficult to envision. Pine forests stood along the coast. Westerly breezes bore their telltale scent far out to sea, which mariners took as a certain sign of their nearing the Virginia coast. William Strachey commented on the effect in 1610, observing "that before we come in sight of it [i.e., Virginia] we smell a sweet savour as is usually from off Cape Vincent, the South Cape of Spayne, if the wind come from the Shoare."[5] Farther inland there were great stands of walnut, hickory, oak, chestnut, elm, beech, poplar, and dozens of other species, whose density was such that it choked off the undergrowth. Large as these forests were, they did not encompass all of the land. A good deal of it lay open naturally. Meadows, dunes, river bottoms, marshes, or tidal flats punctuated the landscape, as did the fields the

Indians had cleared. Numerous and unnamed species of plants, from grasses to flowers to edibles to medicinals, flourished in these open spaces. On land and in water, animal life thrived in kinds and quantities that no English colonist had ever seen. "As for Fish, both of Fresh and Salt-Water, of Shell-Fish, and others," Beverley proclaimed, "no Country can boast of more Variety, greater Plenty, or of better in their several Kinds."[6] Other observers were equally emphatic in their recollections of mammoth flocks of migratory fowl, huge herds of beasts, or strange new creatures like the flying squirrel or the opossum.

Among the odder of the English discoveries, at least to the colonists, were the Indians. These native Virginians, "whose likeliness seemed men to bee," alternately attracted and repelled the settlers. Their innate prejudices against anyone who was neither English nor Christian kept them from seeing the Indians as anything but inferior barbarians.

Depicting the natives as they actually were before 1607 is not an easy task. They had no written languages with which to record their past. Such of their history as they knew, they passed to succeeding generations orally, but these traditions have long since disappeared. Archaeological evidence or the impressions of Europeans survives but each of these sources has its limitations. Archaeology can only tell something of a past

A weroan or great Lorde of Virginia. III.

An Indian Prince or great Lord of Virginia. Other Indians hunt for deer in the background.

civilization's material remains and virtually nothing of its immaterial culture. Seldom did an Englishman put aside his own antipathies toward those he regarded as alien and retell what he witnessed without embellishing upon it so as to make the Indians appear foolish or savage.

Then there is the question of where the Indians belong in the story of Jamestown. Through the years, historians have been willing to leave the formulation of an answer to anthropologists. Recently, however, a desire to highlight the contributions of ethnic Americans has led to a reconsideration of the interplay between Indian and English cultures down to 1700. The prevailing wisdom holds that the natives had a far greater, and by no means negative, effect than was once conceded to them.

No one knows the origins of the Indians, although Virginia was not the land of their ancestors' nativity. Their forebears are thought to have been ancient nomads who wandered across Asia into North America by way of a strip of land that 50,000 years ago bridged the modern Bering Strait. Thereafter, their progeny slowly migrated across the continent, developing as they did different cultural and linguistic traditions, before some of them settled more or less permanently in Virginia. The time of the indians arrival may be fixed with some precision; none of their known sites antedates 9500 B.C. From that date the ancient Virginians' descendants slowly evolved to the point where the generation that lived in the Tidewater as of 1607 was a fairly sedentary people of a varied and complex culture.

Tidewater Indians spoke in tongues that derived from the Algonquian linguistic stock that distinguished them from the natives who lived in the interior of the continent. Their domain was all of Virginia east of the fall line, but there are no accurate tallies of how many lived in that vast territory at the moment of the English landing. Near Jamestown there were, according to John Smith, "some 5000 people, but of able fit men for their warres scarse 1500."[7] Modern estimates put the figure anywhere from double Smith's guess to as many as 170,000. Whatever the correct number may have been, it declined precipitously over the remainder of the seventeenth century. Alcohol, European diseases, loss of homelands, and war devastated the population.

The tribe was the Indians' largest unit of social organization. In 1607, Tidewater was home to some three dozen tribes, all of whom were associated in a loosely knit political organization ruled by the great *werowance*, a man known to the English as Powhatan. Each tribe had its own chief, who was often a woman. In turn, a lesser *werowance* presided over several tribes, and these leaders answered to a council that assisted Powhatan in governing. Ultimately, Powhatan's forceful personality and absolute power gave the entire organization its coherence.

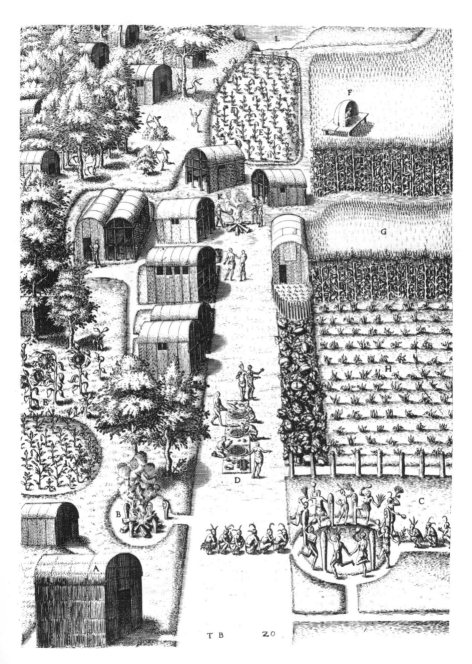

A typical Indian village at the turn of the 17th Century.

25

The Indian manner of making a boat from a solid log.

Individual tribes lived within a defined territory which was theirs to use as they pleased, although none of the members owned land in the same way the English understood ownership. Family groups lived inside palisaded villages "for the most part by the rivers or not farre distant from some fresh spring." Smith continued,

> Their houses are built like our Arbors of small young sprigs bowed and tyed and so close covered with mats or the barkes of trees very handsomely, that notwithstanding either winde raine or weather, they are as warme as stooves, but very smoaky; yet at the toppe of the house there is a hole made for the smoake to goe into right over the fire.[8]

Unlike the English, the Indians traced their lines of kinship through the mother, instead of the father. They held marriage sacred, but they allowed divorce and considered infidelity as the most unforgivable of social offenses. While all Indians had a keen sense of morality and justice, there was no body of accumulated law that equated with England's common law, which the English cherished as the foundation stone of their society. No judges or juries weighed Indian misdeeds or resolved their disputes. Their leaders had the power of life and death, and it was they who chastised the thief, the murderer, or anyone else who broke from tribal customs.

Ritual dances, games, or other ceremonies were an important part of great social occasions such as the harvest or a religious observance. Religious practices were intended to placate the forces of nature, which the English took to be a form of devil worship. Apart from their religious duties, Indian priests were respected for their understanding of illnesses and their cures. Indeed, "Indian physick," as the colonists came to call native remedies, often had greater curative powers than did European medicine.

By 1607, the Indians were adept in taking their living from the land, but they did it in a way that did not unduly disturb the environment's natural balance. The men, who were skilled huntsmen, harvested fish and game with the weir and the community hunt. They designed tools similar to those the English knew, but they fabricated their implements from stone, wood, or bone, rather than steel or iron, both of which were unknown to them. As Smith noted, the natives chose the fertile lowlands as sites for their villages both because the land usually required little clearing and because it was quite fertile. He also described their practice of cultivating large community fields — which the men cleared by slashing and burning — just as he noted how women and children maintained the family plots within the village itself. "They make," he went on to say, "mats, baskets, pots, morters; pound their corne, make their bread, prepare their victuals, plant their corne, gather their corne,

Fish were part of the Indians' diet. Here they are broiled on a rack over an open flame.

beare al kind of burdens, and such like."[9] What the doughty Englishman disparaged was actually a well-defined division of labor in a society that put great store in agricultural labor.

The Indians raised beans, corn, melons, and tobacco. Their skills were such that they frequently grew as many as three crops of corn during a single season. That degree of productivity resulted from their practice of hilling their crops, which they planted in rows. Their method not only produced plants with strong stalks and root systems but it also reduced weeds and contributed to the retention of moisture. Moreover, sowing crops of beans between corn rows helped to revitalize the soil and reduce the need for constantly clearing more fields. These techniques were foreign to the English in 1607, and more than a century passed before they adapted such practices to their own uses.

The arrival of aliens intent on colonizing Virginia presented the Indians with profoundly vexing questions for which there were no pat answers: What did the English have that they wanted? How should they respond to the strangers' presence? Was it possible to retain their cultural integrity or must their culture be subsumed to that of the whites? As the Indians discovered all too soon, the choice of answers was not always theirs to make.

Contrary to what the English thought, or hoped, the natives did not find them intimidating. White men first began probing the Chesapeake coast in the 1520s. There were later occasional contacts when mariners guided their vessels into the bay to look for a safe anchorage where they might rest and reprovision. Jesuit missionaries from Spain tried to raise converts, but they abandoned the attempt in the early 1570s. A short while later, Powhatan learned of the Ralegh expeditions to Roanoke Island. (When his men slaughtered the Chesapeake tribe in 1606, they may also have killed survivors of the Lost Colony who had gone to live with the Chesapeakes.) Captain Newport was no stranger either, for he had met some of the Powhatans when he scouted the bay in the 1590s. The result of such experiences was a healthy caution, and so, in 1607, the Indians of Tidewater greeted these newest strangers warily.

At first, the English posed no threat. They were few, and death carried them off almost as quickly as they came. Consequently, Powhatan, believing that they would soon give up, was content to let them be. Until they left, they seemed to have their limited uses. The English appeared eager to trade tools, pots, cloth, and occasionally firearms for food, fur, or knowledge of how to raise corn or tobacco. With luck, they might also be cajoled into fighting Powhatan's enemies. As far as Powhatan could tell, these were about all of the possibilities, and so he resolved to watch the English in order to discover any other benefits that might inure from a prolonged relationship with them. Events proved the folly of that policy, whereupon the Indians turned hostile toward the whites. Their determination to expel the English from their homeland led to a seventy-five year war of attrition that ended in their almost complete destruction as a people. Today, the offspring of the survivors live on reservations in New Kent and King William counties.

And what of the English? How did the settlers take to Virginia? What were the effects of an unfamiliar world upon them? First of all, they felt relieved at having safely passed across the ocean. An Atlantic crossing tried the endurance of landsmen who had no experience of traveling the high seas in ways they could not imagine. There was the uncertainty of being prisoner to seemingly endless expanses of ocean. There were the terrors of fickle winds that hardly stirred at all or nearly blew a ship beneath mountainous swells. There was the boredom of long voyages. There were the miserable accommodations aboard ships with holds so tiny that every inch of space was precious and so unsanitary that sickness and death were ever-present.

The relief at being in Virginia was momentary because the colonists then had to endure what came to be called "the seasoning"; that is, they had to adapt to a world that differed from the familiar surroundings of home and kin in fundamental ways. Seasoning took time. It was never easy. Some would-be colonists never made the adjustment. Of these, a few gave up and returned to England. Most just gave in to starvation, illness, or loneliness and died. Seasoned colonists saw in their survival signs of divine blessing, which led them to believe that they and their children were chosen of God to prosper in a land without bounds.

Chapter 3

"These Are They Which Came Out of Great Tribulation:"

The Struggle to Survive

The landing at Jamestown was timely. Each of the eager colonists had long since tired of life aboard ship, and the entire company was anxious to get down to the job of settlement. Whatever trials of establishing a new colony might hold for them, nothing could surpass the tribulations of living months at sea with illness, bad food, and close confinement, or so they believed. Then too, some hoped, the tasks of exploring and starting the colony might well stop the leaders from spatting with each other as they had done ever since the ships sailed from Blackwall Dock.

Apparently, the bickering originated with Edward Maria Wingfield and John Smith. Never a reticent man, Smith had offended the highborn and well-connected Wingfield, who took the captain's ready opinions as a sign of disrespect for his betters. Close quarters magnified the frictions between the two so that by the time the fleet had raised the Canaries, they were at a flash point. Wingfield instigated his antagonist's arrest on suspicion of mutiny, and for the duration of the voyage, Smith remained in confinement while his fate was debated. However much Wingfield may have wished to send Smith home to England, or better, have him hanged, his wishes were not to be. Once the ships were in the James, and Newport had opened the London Company's sealed instructions, Smith's appointment to the resident council was revealed. Somehow both men would have to get along. Try as they might, their differences were too great to bridge permanently.

Their quarrel credited no one, but it signified less for either man's reputation than it did for Virginia's future. It symbolized an elemental contentiousness among the leaders at home and in the New World. That discord continued to plague the colony throughout all the years the London Company managed Virginia, just as it led to the company's eventual dissolution.

Acting on the company's instructions, the resident council (with the exception of Smith) — Newport, Captain Gosnold, Wingfield, John Martin, John Ratcliffe, George Kendall — was sworne on May 13, and "Maister *Wingfield* was chosen President."[1] Wingfield followed his election with a debate over what should be done with Smith. He succeeded in keeping him off the council. When the meeting adjourned, Newport, as his orders required, surrendered his command of the expedition to the president.

Every man fell to "worke" over the next few weeks. Newport picked twenty-one men including Smith, George Percy, and Gabriel Archer, and spent six days exploring up the James. The explorers stopped off at the

31

Twenty-one men explored up the James River and stopped off at Indian villages.

Indian villages along the riverbank, where they were more or less cordially received. They pushed on until they came to the Falls of the James. Situated on one of the islands just below the falls, probably Mayo's Island, they found "the habitatyion of the greate kyng Pawatah (i.e., Powhatan)."[2] Powhatan treated the strangers to a feast; they returned the favor, but they could not persuade him to furnish guides to lead them beyond the falls. A frustrated Newport pointed the shallop toward Jamestown, and it was on this leg of their adventure that the colonists met Powhatan's half-brother Opechancanough for the first time.

The men who remained at Jamestown set about unloading the ships and settling down. One gang "cut downe trees to make a place to pitch their Tents," while others laid out gardens and made nets. Another crew cut a cargo of clapboard and sassafras root "to relade the ships." All took time from their labors to attend services of Holy Communion conducted by the Rev. Robert Hunt, who had gone to Virginia in place of the expedition's titular rector, Richard Hakluyt the Younger. For a church, Smith recalled how at first "wee did hang an awning (which is an old saile) to three or foure trees to shadow us from the Sunne, our walles were rales of wood, our seates unhewed trees till we cut plankes, our Pulpit a bar of wood nailed to two neighboring trees. In foule weather we shifted into and old rotten tent." Later, he continued, "wee built a homely thing like a barne, set upon Cratchets (i.e., forked poles), covered with rafts, sedge, and earth."[3] In these lowly accommodations the Church of England struck root in Virginia.

Wingfield at first "would admit no exercise at armes, or fortification but the boughs of trees cast together in the forme of a halfe moone."[4] His reluctance to fortify the encampment arose from a concern that he might violate the company's injunction not to "offend the naturals."[5] A sudden attack, that ended only after the English turned the ships' cannon on the Indians, soon changed Wingfield's mind: he ordered the construction of a stout fort. The work proceeded apace, and by "the fifteenth day of June," as George Percy later told it, "we had built and finished our Fort which was triangle wise, having three Bulwarkes at every corner like a halfe Moone, and foure or five pieces of Artillerie mounted in them."[6]

As June lengthened toward July, the colony appeared settled enough to permit Newport's departure for England to fetch more colonists and supplies. The last of the clapboards and the sassafras, plus some dirt thought to contain gold ore, was packed into the holds of the *Susan Constant* and the *Godspeed*. (The *Discovery* would stay behind.) Weighing anchor on the 22nd, the two vessels sailed off. If there were any disappointment in the admiral, it lay with his cargo. Newport, the colonists, and the backers in London expected the first shipment from Virginia to be more exotic and valuable than tree roots and lumber. Still, there was cause for optimism. The colony, Newport would report to the company, appeared to thrive.

Appearances at Jamestown were deceiving. From the time Newport left Virginia until he returned six months later, Jamestown's situation went from hopeful to hopeless. The other councilors realized their mistake in electing Wingfield president. For all of his courage and dedication, the man could not lead, and his constant sniping at Smith only deepened his colleagues' divisions about Jamestown's future. Worse still, the others accused him of hoarding supplies, and those accusations finally led to his overthrow. Tensions abated after John Ratcliffe's election, though it did not end the whispers of conspiracies. One such plot was the cause of George Kendall's expulsion from the council and his being shot for a Spanish spy. Disease, starvation, and death compounded the divisions. Instead of allowing time to season themselves, the colonists at once plunged into the arduous work of settlement. They were no more careful of their supplies, which they consumed without regard to conserving enough to sustain them until Newport brought more. Foodstuffs were critically short by midsummer. A little barley and wheat remained, and though infested with vermin, it was rationed out in pitifully small portions. Ale supplies dried up as well, and that shortage drove the men to drink from the marsh or the James. The brackish water turned their stomachs as it diseased them. When the balmy days of spring gave over to the heat of an oppressively humid Tidewater summer, the weather only added to the distress.

The outcome of the colonists' situation was as predictable as it was

George Percy

swift. George Percy vividly described what happened. "Our men," he explained,

> "were destroyed with cruell diseases as Swellings, Flixes, Burning Fevers, and by warres, and some departed suddenly, but for the most part they died of meere famine. There was never Englishmen left in a forreigne Countrey in such miserie as wee were in this new discovered Virginia."[7]

Half of Percy's fellow colonists died before September. Fall came and there was relief in the form of cooler weather and the Indians' ripening crops, but despite the natives' generosity, the Englishmen continued to die. When Newport reappeared in January 1608 with the so-called first supply of food and settlers, only thirty-eight of the original complement of colonists survived.

The wonder was that the English perished in the midst of a place that by their own recognition abounded in edible plants and wildlife. Sickly men were obviously too weak to live off the land, but the colonists' debility only partly explains their failure to succor themselves by killing game or catching fish. Cutting back Jamestown's forests diminished the habitat, and the animals went elsewhere. Besides, as any modern outdoorsman knows, guns and nets do not hunters and fishermen make. The cruel truth was that few colonists could either hunt or fish; Smith admitted as much in a letter he sent to the company. "Though there be fish in the Sea, foules in the ayre, and Beasts in the woods," he remarked, "their bounds are so large, they so wild, and we so weake and ignorant, we cannot much trouble them."[8]

Within five or six days of Newport's return, Jamestown caught fire. The blaze consumed the fort, the storehouse, and all but three dwellings. Newport helped with the reconstruction, and for a time his presence had a calming effect on the council. As rations again grew short, however, he realized the necessity of his leaving for England. He stayed through the first week of April, and when he left, he took Wingfield and Gabriel Archer with him.

Newport was back in Virginia in October. This second supply contained seventy immigrants, as well as a fresh cargo of supplies. These latest arrivals included Germans and Poles, some of whom were instrumental in starting a glass factory on the north mainland at what is now called "Glass House Point." There were also two women, the colony's first. One was a "Mistress *Forrest*"; the other was her maidservant, Anne Burras. A short while later, "there was a marriage betwixt *John Laydon* and *Anne Burras*; which was the first marriage we had in Virginia."[9]

Neither Newport's presence nor the departure of Archer and Wingfield resolved the fundamental problem of leadership. With the exception of Smith, none of the remaining councilors was up to the responsibility. The indolent Ratcliffe proved every bit as disagreeable and inept as his predecessor. When his term as president expired in September 1608, a majority of the council prevailed upon Smith to succeed him.

Assuredly one of the outstanding early colonists, John Smith is as much the object of dispute today as when he lived. Smith possessed a confidence in his ability that came from wide experience as a soldier of fortune, and he was seldom shy in sharing his opinions, whether solicited or not. His contemporaries found his propensity to brag offensive. Indeed, the well-born among them often took it as a sign of an upstart who did not defer to his betters. Modern scholars regard many of his Virginia escapades, which cannot be confirmed by accounts separate from his own, as the embroideries of a colorful tale teller. His vivid prose still entertains, even if its accuracy is subject to doubt. Smith's standing as an historian may be shaky, but his place as a colonizer is not. Without Smith, Jamestown would have come nearer to ruin than it did.

Smith's emergence began soon after the Rev. Mr. Hunt engineered his restoration to the council in the summer of 1607. A few months later,

Near the site of the original Glasshouse, a reconstruction of a typical 17th Century building was erected in 1956.

At the Glasshouse craftsmen demonstrate the art of glassblowing.

Many different glass products are offered for sale.

Captain John Smith

Ratcliffe appointed him supply master, which afforded him the opportunity to trade with the Indians. He applied his talents for diplomacy to stockpile enough food to ease the shortages. In the course of his dealings, he became the colonists' most experienced negotiator. When Smith was not trading, he was off exploring. In December 1607, while scouting up the Chickahominy River, a party of Powhatan's warriors caught him. They held him captive for several weeks. Resourceful man that Smith was, he kept his captors from killing him by showing off a pocket compass and amusing them with tall tales and bold threats. These contrivances eventually ceased to amuse the Indians, who resolved to kill their captive in Powhatan's presence. Several men forced Smith's head down on a stone, "and being ready with their clubs, to beate out his brains, *Pocahontas* the Kings dearest daughter, when no intreaty could prevaile, got his head in her armes, and laid her owne upon his to save him from death: whereat the Emperour was contented that he should live."[10] Because of their respect for him, the Indians set him free.

Smith's captivity had proved beneficial for the English because as long as the intrepid captain stayed in Virginia the "naturals" remained friendly. He came closer to death upon his return to Jamestown in January 1608. His enemies on the council tried to hang him for the loss of two of his men, but Newport's timely arrival spared him the noose. After the fire, he helped Newport and the others begin the rebuilding of Jamestown. Smith then spent most of the spring and summer exploring and mapping the upper reaches of Chesapeake Bay. He was elected president when he returned to the settlement in September.

Soon after Smith assumed his duties, Newport dropped anchor off Jamestown with the second supply. This supply of new settlers hardly pleased the president; of the seventy who shipped over, half were gentlemen. True, the remainder was an assortment of artisans and laborers, but there were no husbandmen who might turn their knowledge of agriculture to raising food. Moreover, Newport brought new orders from company officials. They instructed him to go to Powhatan and crown him, on the theory that his coronation would subjugate him to English rule and validate the company's claim to Virginia. Newport was also to go beyond the Falls of the James to seek out Powhatan's enemies and question them as to the whereabouts of the Roanoke Island colonists. Finally, the admiral was to search for gold and the South Sea. None of these instructions filled Smith with joy, but soldier that he was, he knew they must be obeyed.

John Smith traded with the Indians.

Pocahontas (in 1616)

Newport and Smith went off to Powhatan's main village, where they were cordially met. Gifts were exchanged, "but a fowle trouble there was to make [Powhatan] kneele to receave his crowne."[11] Contrary to the English understanding, Powhatan knew well the meaning of the ceremony. He refused to bend his knee to the foreigners, though they did succeed in bending him low enough for Newport to put the circlet round his head. In exchange for this "gift," Powhatan gave Newport an old pair of shoes and a cloak, which certainly were no symbols of his submission. The "coronation" complete, Newport's party trekked beyond the Falls of the James until they came upon the Monacans, who confirmed what the Powhatans had already averred: there were no survivors from Roanoke. Of course, the party discovered neither gold nor the South Sea.

Smith could scarcely conceal his exasperation at spending valuable time in search of wills-o'-the-wisp. When Newport sailed for England in December, he carried only a cargo of lumber and a curt letter from the president. Smith upbraided company officials for their own unrealistic expectations as well as their failure to provide him with competent laborers. "When you send againe," he remarked tartly, "I intreate you rather send but thirty Carpenters, husbandmen, gardiners, fisher men, blacksmiths, masons, and diggers up of trees, roots, well provided; then a thousand of such as we have; for except wee be able both to lodge them, and feed them, the most will consume with want of necessaries before they can be made good for any thing." The latter sort, he concluded, could never satisfy the company's "desire of present profit."[12]

In spite of the irritations, Smith managed the colony well. He had begun improvements to Jamestown before the second supply's arrival, and with Newport's sailing, he put the men back to building houses. As the weather chilled, the men finished digging a well and stockpiled enough corn to last the winter. The corn rotted, but Smith prevented another famine by sending Jamestown's inhabitants to live in the outposts at Old Point Comfort and the falls. That winter of 1608-1609 was hard, the colonists suffered, but most of them lived to greet the spring.

Smith also attacked the problem of indolent, carping colonists. In his mind, military discipline was the surest cure for laziness and complaining. First, he organized the men into companies and taught them the use of weapons. He then daily drilled the companies in the manual of arms, which increased both their skill and discipline. Only the sick were exempt from the regular routines of work and drill. His scheme succeeded, and it gave the small colony an order that it had heretofore missed. Not only that, but the sight of healthy, well-drilled English soldiers served as a caution to the natives.

Throughout the spring of 1609, Smith worked his gangs in preparing cargoes for the expected ships from England. None came until mid-July, when a lone vessel straggled into the anchorage at Sandy Bay. It bore Samuel Argall and Smith's old enemies on the council, Archer, Martin, and Ratcliffe. Argall had news of the impending arrival of a third supply and a reorganization of the colony's government. The latter intelligence touched off the dissidents anew, and they attempted to overthrow Smith. They were unsuccessful until an accidental gunpowder explosion greviously wounded him. An injured Smith proved a safe target for his enemies, who deposed him and replaced him with George Percy. Sorely needing medical attention, Smith left for England in October.

Smith never returned to Jamestown, but he left his mark nonetheless. He salvaged the colony at a critical moment in its short existence. His use of military discipline anticipated company policy. His practice of intimidating the Indians into cooperation remained the settlers' basic tactic toward the natives for years to come. For all of that, nothing Smith accomplished answered the fundamental questions of the best way to convert Virginia to profitable uses or which Englishmen had the best skills to make the conversion.

Investors in the London Company expected that they would recover their investment in the Jamestown venture within two years of the colony's founding. Confirmation of that belief seemed to come from Newport when he returned home for the first supply. He gave a glowing account of what he had seen, commenting in a letter to the Earl of Salisbury that "the Contrie is excellent and verie Riche in gold and Copper."[13] His cargo, especially the ore samples, heightened expectations; nevertheless, prospects for quick rewards were soon dimmed. The ore contained no gold, but more to the point, the Londoners were distressed by the reports of how little at Jamestown had gone according to their plans. Disheartened but still convinced of the colony's potential value, company members carefully reexamined the entire operation during the winter of 1608-1609. The result of their review was the decision to reorganize the company in fundamental ways, and that required a new charter from the crown.

King James I granted the new charter early in 1609. It revised the company's corporate arrangements, it streamlined the government at Jamestown, and it empowered the company to sell its stock publicly. The old royal council was abolished. In its place were a treasurer and a council, whom the stockholders elected to manage affairs from London. A governor would replace the president at Jamestown. He served at the company's pleasure, though he could select subordinate officers, including his own council of advisers.

The stock sale met with an extraordinarily enthusiastic response from City merchants and other public-spirited men as some fifty-six of the London guilds and more than six hundred individuals bought into the new company. Heartened by this show of support, the newly elected treasurer, Sir Thomas Smythe, and his colleagues planned Jamestown's revival. Choosing a new governor was among the first orders of business, and they selected a former Privy Councilor, Thomas West, Lord De la Warr. De la Warr had soldiered on the continent, he possessed the political and military training that company officials now believed was required to make Jamestown a paying concern. The company hired a pair of soldiers, Sir Thomas Gates and Sir Thomas Dale as his assistants. Smythe next turned to finding, ships, supplies, and colonists. He recruited five hundred willing men, women, and children, whose passage he booked on nine vessels that sailed for Virginia in May 1609.

Because De la Warr's affairs prevented the governor from leaving with the convoy, he gave over command to Gates. Gates, Sir George Somers, the fleet's admiral, and Christopher Newport quarreled over precedence. They settled the argument by agreeing to sail aboard the flagship *Sea Venture*, instead of sailing separately. That decision turned into a costly

Thomas West, Lord De la Warr

mistake.

An unfavorable wind held the convoy on the English coast for weeks. When it finally shifted, it blew stormy for much of the voyage. There was an outbreak of plague that killed dozens of would-be colonists. A hurricane hit the convoy off the shore of the West Indies, sinking a ketch with all hands and wrecking the *Sea Venture* on the Bermuda coast, though her passengers survived. Now the folly of Gates, Somers, and Newport all sailing together on the flagship was revealed; a leaderless fleet strayed into the James and dropped anchor at Jamestown in August.

The landing of four hundred new settlers was no cause for celebration. There was not enough time to raise more food for the extra mouths; the growing season was near its end. The rigors of their crossing weakened everyone to the point that no one was healthy enough to ward off further disease, or to prepare for the coming winter. All these latest arrivals could do was eat, and in doing that, they drew down the colony's limited stores, as piercingly cold weather broke across the Tidewater and famine set in. Those who could, staved off starvation by eating nuts, roots, acorns, horsehide — or worse. A survivor recalled that

> a Salvage we slew and buried, the poorer sort tooke him up
> againe and eat him; and so did divers others one another

boyled with roots and herbs: And one amongst the rest did kill his wife, powdered [i.e., salted] her, and had eaten part of her before it was knowne; for which hee was executed, as hee well deserved: now whether shee was better roasted, boyled or carbonado'd [i.e., grilled], I know not; but such a dish as powdered wife I never heard of.[14]

At length, death claimed the starving, as it relieved those visited with typhoid or dysentery. The winter of 1609-1610 was long remembered as "that time . . . we called the starving time; it were too vile to say, and scarce to be beleeved, what we endured."[15] Of five hundred colonists who were living in the fall, a mere sixty lasted into spring.

In Bermuda, Gates, John Rolfe, and the *Sea Venture*'s other survivors scavenged the wreck's useable tackle, built two pinnaces from timber they cut on the island, and then sailed for Jamestown. When they landed there in May 1610, Gates believed the colony was beyond repair, and he decided to abandon it. He wasted little time in loading up the survivors. The sad fleet was on its way down the James when word came that Lord De la Warr was in the bay. His lordship's arrival in the nick of time saved Jamestown, at least temporarily.

De la Warr acted at once to put things in order. Following the example set by John Smith, he assigned everyone to a rigid work schedule that required the performance of specific duties, and he got results. Accounts

"The Day of Providence," June 10, 1610, the arrival of Lord De la Warr with new settlers and ample supplies saved Jamestown.

of his successes sired the hope in London that Jamestown at last verged on profitability, but with the governor's sudden reappearance in England, hopefulness was dashed. Never a well man, De la Warr found conditions at Jamestown too demanding of his delicate constitution, and in March 1611, he hurried home to amend his health. His report of conditions in the colony was dispiriting because it told of little but death and Indian troubles.

While De la Warr's news disheartened Smythe, he refused to let despair overtake him. Instead, he turned anew to Gates and Dale, both of whom had gone to England ahead of De la Warr. He dispatched them back to Virginia with new responsibilities. Gates would become governor while Dale would hold a newly created office of marshall. Dale's post came directly from English military practices. In an English army of the time, the marshall was responsible for maintaining discipline after the fashion of martial law. Rather than subjecting the colony to martial law per se, however, company leaders entrusted Dale with a set of stringent regulations that mixed together military and civilian legal practices. (They became known as The *Lawes Divine, Morall and Martiall* following their publication by William Strachey in 1612.) The appointment of Dale and the promulgation of the *Lawes* were indicative of the company's intent to impose a military model of organization on its struggling colony.

Gates and Dale complemented one another, and they proved the equals of their tasks during their five-year administration. A stern disciplinarian, Dale held the colonists to the very letter of the *Lawes*, and his rigor eventually made them tractable. The marshall and the governor improved living conditions at Jamestown, they opened new settlements along the James, they encouraged experimentation with crops of potential market value, and they even allowed a measure of private land ownership. They also succeeded in pacifying the natives, especially after 1613 when Samuel Argall took Pocahontas for a hostage. This "unbeleeving creature" converted to Christianity and won the "hartie and best thoughts" of John Rolfe, whom she married.[16] In spite of these accomplishments, which were considerable, Gates and Dale brought Jamestown no nearer to profitability than had any of their predecessors. No one had yet found that one commodity that could turn a struggling colony into a thriving business.

Enter John Rolfe.

He knew the English fondness for tobacco; he was himself addicted to it. The rage for smoking had grown steadily ever since some of Ralegh's colonists introduced the habit back in the 1580s. Ralegh himself smoked, and he made the practice acceptable among the fashionable swells at Queen Elizabeth's court. Trouble was, however, that the main source of

John Rolfe experimented with tobacco planting for two years before he produced his first four barrels of cured leaf.

tobacco was the sweet-scented leaf that grew only in the Spanish Indies. When available, it was immediately snapped up by eager consumers who willingly paid handsome prices for even the smallest of pipefuls. Ironically enough, English agriculturalists knew that tobacco would grow in the British Isles. In the early 1600s, some even published tracts on how to raise it, but few landowners followed their advice. Once in the Tidewater, the English discovered the natives using tobacco in their ceremonies, although the smoking colonists scorned the Indians' variety. The Virginia plant, *Nicotiana rustica*, produced a thick, smallish leaf with a biting taste when smoked.

Rolfe saw prosperity in these seemingly unconnected bits of information. Therein lay his genius and his everlasting effect on Jamestown, the colony of Virginia, and the future United States. If the Indians raised tobacco, he reasoned, so could he, but instead of the stubby local plant, he planned to grow the desirable West Indian species, *Nicotiana tabacum*. Gates and Dale urged him on with his experiments. The problem was to discover which strains of the West Indian leaf he could adapt to Virginia cultivation and how a crop might be cured for transport to English markets. Success was not instanteous. Rolfe experimented for more than two years before he produced his first four barrels of cured leaf, which Gates took with him when he returned to England in 1614. At last, Rolfe had found something, which in the words of a fellow colonist, Ralph Hamor, "everyman may plant, and with the least part of his labour, tend and cure will returne him both cloaths and other necessaries."[17]

The rest of the story is a familiar tale. Rolfe's fellow colonists took up tobacco planting with utter abandon. In their feverish effort to emulate Rolfe, they planted the stuff everywhere, even in "the market-place, and the streets, and all the other spare places" about Jamestown.[18] More than 50,000 pounds of the leaf were shipped home by 1618; the best of it commanded 3s a pound. The first American boom was on, and Jamestown's future was assured. That was John Rolfe's achievement.

Smythe and other London Company officials did not see salvation in tobacco. They still believed the key to redeeming the company's investment depended upon the development of other more desirable staples. Besides, they knew that King James I abominated smoking. And yet, without meaning to, they ensured the development of a tobacco-based economy. In 1616, they declared a promised dividend in land, instead of cash, thereby reinforcing Gates's own limited introduction of private landownership. Private tenure came to Virginia in 1617, when the company instituted the headright system. This scheme attracted settlers with its promise 50 of acres of land to anyone who bought his passage, as well as an additional 50 acres for every other person he brought to Virginia at his own expense. In effect, because these changes enabled individual colonists to acquire their own land and laborers, they heightened, rather than diminished, tobacco's attractiveness.

Unaccustomed to the exertions of deep thought, avaricious would-be planters never pondered the consequences of copying Rolfe. Within a matter of years, tobacco culture transformed Virginia into a place where the fortunate few could free themselves from the restraints of English society and aggrandize themselves by the labors of others. As they scratched their way to the top of Virginia's emerging society, such men cursed the colony with a single-crop economy whose indentured servants and slave laborers were its very foundation.

No celebration marked Jamestown's tenth anniversary; no one in the London Company had any cause to celebrate in 1617. The company was a deeply troubled business that neared collapse. Everything about Virginia confounded expectations. The expenses of maintaining the colony exceeded the wildest estimates, and there was never enough cash in the company coffers. Neither the stock issue of 1609 nor the lottery authorized by another charter revision in 1612 alleviated the cash shortage. Colonists died faster than they could be recruited. Those who lived complained too loudly, ate too much, and produced too little. While Virginia was by every account a fascination for all who beheld it, it had no gold mines or the new route to the Indies. All these issues compounded to raise doubts in the minds of stockholders who wondered if they would ever recover their investments, not to mention profit from them. Their uncertainties undermined Smythe and wedged rival factions

The London Company conducted lotteries to raise cash for the colony.

further apart.

Bad as things seemed, no one, officer or stockholder, was prepared to give up on Virginia. Too much was at stake. In 1618 the London Company pulled itself together to mount one more try. Stockholders who had pinned their hopes on Sir Edwin Sandys cast Smythe aside and elected Sir Edwin treasurer. One of Smythe's more vocal critics, Sandys had long argued the wisdom of broad reforms in the Jamestown operation. Profit, he contended, lay in getting the colonists to produce staples that had ready markets in England. (In his opinion, tobacco was not to be one of these.) Further, he judged that Virginia was unattractive to the "right" kinds of colonists so long as it remained in the nature of a military outpost. Good people would only go over if the company inspired the transfer of as much of England's traditional social order as the wilderness and the colonists' own inclinations would permit. As company treasurer, Sandys had the power to act on his ideas. He incorporated them in commissions and instructions that collectively came to be styled the "Great Charter." They included the substitution of rules akin to local English law for The *Lawes Divine, Morall and Martiall*, an improved local administration, a more representative governing authority, and new forms of landholding. To entice seasoned colonists into becoming subsidiary developers, Sandys promised generous grants of land and political authority. That scheme gave rise to "particular plantations," settlements whose promoters gave their grants fancy-sounding names such as Berkeley, Bermuda, or Flowerieu Hundred. The last element in Sandys's grand design was a liberal infusion of new supplies and settlers that included a contingent of single women. Sandys entrusted his plans to an old Virginia hand, George Yeardley, for whom he secured a knighthood.

Upon his arrival, Sir George issued writs for an election of leading colonists to meet with him in an assembly at Jamestown. Twenty-two were elected; they and their successors who would be known until 1775 as burgesses. Assembling on July 30, 1619, the burgesses met with Yeardley and his six councilors in the "Quire of the Churche," which was the only place large enough to accommodate them all.[19] Everyone swore the oaths of allegiance and supremacy to the crown, whereupon Governor Yeardley appointed Secretary of the Colony John Pory speaker, and the members of this first General Assembly got down to business.

They first examined the burgesses' qualifications. Two of the burgesses were ejected pending clarification of their land patents from London. The Assembly then moved on to legislative matters, putting some of Yeardley's instructions into law, petitioning the company to make changes in the Great Charter, and passing its own laws on Indian relations, the price of tobacco, and indentured servants. The Assembly next took up some criminal cases, but their dispatch was cut short on August 4. "This daye," reads Pory's journal, "(by reason of extream heate paste and most likely to ensue and by that meanes of the alteration of the healthes of diverse of the general Assembly) the Governour, who himself also was not well, resolved should be the last of this first

The first General Assembly at Jamestown, July 30, 1619.

49

Pocahontas married John Rolfe in April 1614.

session."[20] Brief though it was, it set a precedent for the gradual development of self-government and representative political institutions in Virginia and elsewhere in English America.

Precedents were of little interest either to the first General Assembly or to Sir Edwin Sandys — turning a profit was. For a time, Sir Edwin's roll of the dice seemed like a winner. The lure of cheap land and Sandys's aggressive recruiting of settlers, especially women, children, and a few families, swiftly swelled the colony's population. Agricultural production increased. Customary legal, social, and political usages were transplanted, and so began the slow process of their adaptation to a new setting. However encouraging were these things none of them came quickly enough to relieve the company of its fiscal distress. Then too, Sandys himself was the target of continual sniping. Sir Thomas Smythe's loyalists lost no opportunity to tax Sandys for failing to redeem his promise to amend the company's ills. Their attacks led an exasperated James I to withdraw the lottery privilege, and its loss stopped the company's only steady flow of capital. The worst was yet to come. London was abuzz in the late spring of 1622 with tales of a sudden Indian attack upon the unsuspecting and unprepared colonists.

Long years of peace lulled the settlers into carelessly believing that they and Powhatan's people might live together in harmony. Relations had been calm ever since Powhatan had agreed in 1614 to refrain from attacking the English, and his daughter's wedding to John Rolfe symbolized the tranquility between red men and white. The Indians labored, however, under a different perception of reality. The English contempt for their ways angered them. Little in what they had learned about English culture attracted them, except for fire arms and trade goods. In the end, the indians came to see the growth of English settlements for what it had become, a menace to their existence as a race of free people.

How to meet the threat? That question sorely vexed the Indians because its answers were so few. Peace was one option. That way led to the loss of more land. Assimilation on English terms was another alternative. That course meant the loss of identity. They could move west of the English settlements. That choice would lead to conflicts with enemy tribes. They could war on the English. No one knows how much Powhatan and his subordinates may have debated these possibilities before 1622. But for as long as Pocahontas and Powhatan lived, the natives continued friendly even to the point of acceding to increased encroachments on their territory or converting to Christianity.

Pocahontas, John Rolfe, and Thomas, their infant son, went to England in 1616. The Indian princess took the fancy of London's fashionable set. Sadly, she died a year later as the Rolfes prepared to sail for Virginia. Pocahontas's father joined his ancestors in 1618, whereupon his brother Itopatin was chosen chief werowance. Opechancanough replaced him a short while later. His elevation boded ill for the English.

All of the Indians who knew Opechancanough well also knew of his passion for destroying the English. However much he wished to be rid of the English, the new great werowance was too crafty to allow emotion to cloud his judgment. Haste would confound any likelihood of attaining his goal. His only chance of success lay in suddenly, massively, and simultaneously assaulting the entire line of enemy settlements. Such a bold stroke demanded time and secrecy of planning, as well as coordination and the proper moment of execution. Accordingly, Opechancanough schemed in private as he surreptitiously amassed his warriors. He pretended friendship with English all the while, even vowing that the heavens should fall before *he* would break the peace.

He struck on March 22, 1622, a day, as he correctly calculated, when the English would be the most unsuspecting. "And by this meanes that fatall Friday morning," according to a lurid contemporary account,

> there fell under the bloudy and barbarous hands of that perfidious and inhumane people, contrary to all lawes of God and men, of Nature and Nations, three hundred forty seven men, women, and children, most by their own weapons; and not being content with taking away life alone, they fell after againe upon the dead, making as well as they could, a fresh

51

In March 1622, Opechananough and his warriors struck the English settlements and killed about one-third of the colony's population.

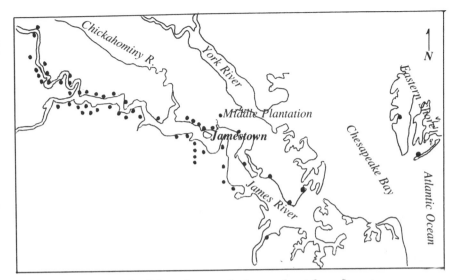

By 1622, English settlements had spread out from Jamestown (center) and extended all the way up the James River to the falls (top left).

murder, defacing, dragging, and mangling the dead carkasses into many pieces, and carrying some parts away in derision, with base and brutish triumph."[21]

That loss accounted for one-third of the colony's population. Jamestown escaped destruction only because the inhabitants got wind of the coming blow.

Opechancanough failed to press the attack vigorously, but what the English would call the "massacre," as well as more raids, sickness, and starvation almost undid the colony. When the English overcame their disarray, they struck back, and the fighting turned into a nasty war of attrition that lasted into the late 1620s. It was a fight that counted its costs in more things than lives lost and treasure spent. The Indians had made a choice of war to the death in preference to assimilation or emigration. The colonists were no longer at pains to be friendly with natives who stood in the way of settlement. Thus, the massacre brought the demise of the London Company.

Meeting the demands of Opechancanough's war destroyed the stockholders' will. They grew ever more contentious, and they vented their anger on Sandys, who was by no means blameless. Coupled with his rapid infusion of new colonists into Jamestown, Sandy's overlarge promotions severely strained a colony at war, and they may well have contributed to the outburst of fighting in the first place. Moreover, the colonists raged at the lack of assistance against their enemy. Most damaging to Sandys's leadership was the failure of his schemes to produce any profits. The outcry against the treasurer mounted until the clamor became so loud that it forced the crown to intervene, but royal intervention could not still Sandys's critics. A weary King James then opted for more drastic measures. Acting on James's orders in November 1623, Attorney-General Thomas Coventry sued the London Company in the Court of Kings Bench upon a writ of *quo warranto* to show cause why it should not lose its charter. The resort to law sealed the company's fate. Within six months of Coventry's suit, the court held for the crown, the charter was seized, and the company was no more.

James favored turning Virginia's management over to a reorganized company, but one that he more directly controlled. Seeking advice on how that end might be attained, he named an advisory commission chaired by Henry, Lord Mandeville, the president of the Privy Council. James's untimely death on March 27, 1625 made short shrift of the commission's work. The question of what to do with Virginia fell to the new monarch, Charles I. He found his answer within six weeks of his father's passing. He proclaimed Virginia a royal colony.

Why did the London Company fail?

The explanations are as abundant as they are obvious. Not enough money, bumbling leaders, divided responsibilities, stupid colonists, lazy colonists, disagreements about purposes, fanciful expectations, each of these was part of the calculus of failure. Of course, failure is neither the entire story of the London Company nor its only monument. The company gained an English foothold in North America. It opened a door to the expansion of English trade and commerce. It encouraged the transplantation of English social values, government, and law to an American setting. It laid the first foundations of a new nation. Such are the things that came out of great tribulation.

Chapter 4
Seat of Government

By virtue of its being the first settlement, Jamestown became Virginia's capital, and for nine decades it was the cockpit of politics. Here stood the seat of government. Here presided the king's personal representative, the royal governor. Here sat Virginia's two highest courts. Here burgesses and councilors met with the governor in general assembly to enact "wholesome lawes and statutes."[1] Here men with little experience of dominion over others learned the uses of power, as well as its arts and mysteries. Here is where the American practice of self-government struck root, gained nurturance, and grew into a sacred tradition.

Seventeenth-century Englishmen accepted as natural a political world of unequals in which the privileged few ordered the destinies of the many. There was no toleration of diversity, religious or otherwise. Speaking out freely could be a serious breach of law. In certain circumstances this applied even to private thought; just to "imagine the death of the King, Queen, or Prince" was tantamount to treason.[2] All adults were not automatically enfranchised. No Englishwoman voted. Such a right did not inhere in these "weaker vessels." (Of course, there was also nothing akin to equality between the sexes.) Unless a man owned or rented real property equal to the value of £2 sterling, he too was excluded from voting. The vote gave the voter no warrant to hold office because officeholding was the exclusive prerogative of men of merit. Meritorious men, the theory went, invariably sprang from England's ruling families, and these "natural" leaders were owed the deference of those whom they governed. None of the rulers ever gave a moment's concern for testing the "public's" views on anything. The opinion of ordinary folk meant nothing in the councils of the mighty because "no account [was] made of them."[3]

Throughout the seventeenth century, the contest between king and commoner over who should rule England led the contestants to inquire deeply into these assumptions about the nature of English polity. Such inquiries informed Virginia's emerging self-governing tradition, but they were not its only source. An ocean between Jamestown and London, the distances between the colonists and Jamestown, the desire to seek private gain in an atmosphere freed from Old World restraints, the need for ways to raise taxes, resolve legal disputes, and protect the colonists — these too afforded an ample environment for experimenting with forms of governance and uses of power.

Answering a query from the Privy Council in 1670, Sir William Berkeley wrote of Virginia's government, "There is a governor and sixteen counsellors, . . . judge and determine all causes that are above

King Charles I

fifteen pound sterling; for what is under, there are particular courts in every county which are twenty in number. Every year, at least," he continued, "the assembly is called, before whom lye appeals, and this assembly is composed of two burgesses out of every county. These lay the necessary taxes . . . as their exigencies require."[4] Berkeley's observations accurately portrayed the shape the colony's government had taken by the last third of the century. He offered the Privy Councilors no explanation for how or why it assumed that particular form, and he carefully withheld the extent of the colonists' self-government.

A proper government for Virginia had been one of the London Company's perennial concerns. Initially, the Charter of 1606 gave political authority to a resident council and a president, but that arrangement soon proved unworkable. The Charter of 1609 replaced it with a governor and a council of his hand-picked advisers. Then came the addition of a general assembly, with its measure of home rule. By 1619, the basic outline of Virginia's government was complete. However, the downfall of the company cast a shadow over it because the crown was in no way obliged to retain the colonial government as it stood in 1624.

Like his father, Charles I inclined toward a reconstituted company, but he was slow in reaching a decision. The crown, in the meanwhile, managed Virginia much as the company had done after 1618, and the company's last governor, Sir Francis Wyatt, became Virginia's first royal governor. Wyatt's appointment marked a significant step in the transition from company to royal rule. It provided the excuse to dispel any lingering doubts about the source of public authority in Virginia, and it forced the king's advisers to define the office.

Henceforth, the governors would be crown appointees who held their office at the royal pleasure or until retirement or death removed them. Legally, they would derive their authority from documents known as commissions and instructions. The former empowered the recipient to act in the king's behalf and described his responsibilities; the latter set forth how his duties should be executed. Modeled on similar company documents, the royal commission and instructions eventually became fairly standardized statements of the crown's view of the governor's role in Virginia politics.

Styled "his majesty's governor and captain-general," the chief executive was the king's vice-regent with broad power to implement royal policies. He received an annual salary that was eventually worth £2000, a sum that was considerably augmented by various fees that law and custom bestowed on the governor. He was the fountainhead of justice, favor, as well as commander in chief. The colony's subordinate civil, military, and ecclesiastical officials were either his appointees or his nominees. The General Assembly and the Council of State met at his call. No legislative measure passed into law without his assent; his veto immediately killed any bill he opposed. In theory, the position carried the greatest prestige and power of any political post in the colony. In fact, lack of support from London, customary accretions, and gubernatorial collusion with Virginia politicians diminished the practical authority of the office, but the crown's view of it remained unchanged after 1624: the governor linked the king directly to his subjects in his oldest American dominion.

Judging the contributions of Virginia's seventeenth-century royal governors is no easy task. The lack of records precludes any lengthy assessment of all but a few. Of these, Sir Francis Wyatt, Sir John Harvey, Sir William Berkeley, Thomas Culpeper, Lord Culpeper, and Francis, Lord Howard of Effingham, are the most noteworthy.

A Kentish man, Wyatt sprang from genteel stock deeply rooted in the county's social and political life. His grandfather, Sir Thomas, went to a traitor's death in 1554 for raising Wyatt's Rebellion against Queen Mary Tudor, but his father, George, successfully repaired the family's fortunes and reputation. Francis was knighted in 1618, married a niece of Sir Edwin Sandys. His connections explain why both the London Company and the crown picked him. He was, according to contemporary opinion, "well reputed of, both in respect of his parentage, good education, integritie of life and faire fortunes."[5]

It was also Wyatt's fortune to preside over Virginia in times of emergency. He began his first stint as governor just months before the massacre, which, when it came, surprised him no less than his fellow colonists. Mobilizing the demoralized settlers, while at the same time trying to advance the programs of an equally dispirited company, was an exquisite test for a man who had no practical military or political experience. Wyatt learned his lessons quickly and well. He retained the confidence of his superiors as he engineered Opechancanough's eventual defeat. His skill at stabilizing the Virginians made him the crown's obvious choice as its first governor, and so he guided the colony through the initial stages of royal rule. Wyatt went home in 1626, and for more than a decade, he had no contact with the colony. Charles I recalled him, sending him back to calm a Virginia wracked by internal discord. Once again, Wyatt's good sense and his talents for conciliation, as well as the reforms he instituted, eased the situation for Sir William Berkeley.

One of Wyatt's fellow governors, Sir John Harvey, was at the center of the troubles that bedeviled the colony for most of the 1630s. The colonists had not recovered fully from the effects of the Indian war. Charles I's indecisiveness about the final dispostion of their government made them edgy, especially because his indecision kept the legality of such important things as land titles or the General Assembly very much in doubt. The founding of Maryland within the territorial limits of Virginia raised fears of the Virginians' inundation by the hated papists. Lord Baltimore's ambitions collided with trading rights that the crown had already granted to a most important Virginian, William Claiborne. Claiborne typified a change in the sort of men who ruled in Virginia in the post-company years. In the London Company's day, Virginia's leaders were drawn from traditional ruling classes, but there were fewer of these individuals in the colony after 1624; they either died or went home. In their place came men such as Claiborne whose right to rule rested on no better claim than their ability to survive in the Virginia wilds. Unused to power, they were resentful of any intrusion on their authority, and in their minds, Harvey was a prickly intruder.

To govern Virginia in these conditions was a trial for anyone, but Harvey was a man blessed with talents for making a bad situation worse. A sea captain, the newly knighted Harvey became governor in 1628. Friends characterized Sir John as rigid, but "a proper man, though somewhat choleric and impatient."[6] Upon taking up his government in 1630, he wasted little time before feuding with Claiborne and other members of the Council of State over the extent of his authority to act independently of them. The antagonisms mounted after he made peace with the Indians and assisted the Marylanders through the first difficult days of settlement. Relations approached the flash point when he advanced Lord Baltimore's claims to the upper reaches of the Chesapeake Bay against those of Claiborne and other Virginia fur traders. All of this was too much for the exasperated councilors who, in the spring of 1635, arrested Harvey, charged him with assorted grievances, and packed him off to England. He successfully defended himself, and he eventually won the unenthusiastic support of King Charles who sent him back in 1637. Claiborne and the others lobbied to have him replaced by Sir Francis Wyatt, and in 1639, their efforts finally paid off. Their "thrusting out" of Harvey served notice of their intention to share largely in controlling Virginia's politics, and it opened the door to the rise of the colony's ruling classes. These were lessons that Sir William Berkeley certainly took to heart.

Berkeley's thirty-five year tenure marks him as one of Virginia's most significant colonial chief executives; he was also one of the most controversial. Berkeley stood with that handful who closely identified themselves with leading Virginians and their interests, even when those interests opposed the crown's. His vanity, his hauteur, his stubborness, and his ruthlessness earned him the cautious respect, if not the fear, of those he governed, just as his vindictive suppression of Bacon's Rebellion gained him the hostility of many Virginia historians. Truth to tell,

Sir William Berkeley

59

his was not an endearing personality, but that defect should not be the excuse for ignoring his part in fostering self-government in Virginia.

Born in 1606, Sir William was a younger son of Sir Maurice Berkeley of the prominent Berkeleys of Somerset. His family, their influence with King Charles's court, and his accomplishments won Berkeley the Virginia appointment. Being named governor offered him an opportunity to advance that was often unavailable to younger sons in civil war England. In this respect, he differed not at all from other substantial immigrants of the period; like them, he became a large planter and a leading Virginian. His arrival was also timely for he governed Virginia during the crucial decades from the 1640s to the 1670s. These were the years when the General Assembly matured into a miniature parliament, and political power was divided between the provincial and the county governments. Berkeley encouraged both developments for they comported with his political style. Nevertheless, by sanctioning the growth of colonial autonomy, he weakened his control as well as that of the crown.

The desire to curb such independence led the later Stuarts to send Thomas, Lord Culpeper and Francis, Lord Howard of Effingham to Virginia. Both men shared their royal masters' vision of a well-disciplined empire in which subservient colonists met the needs of the mother country. An impoverished nobleman, Culpeper showed remarkably more adeptness for mending his broken fortunes at the Virginians' expense than he did in advancing the crown's imperial designs. Himself no stranger to penury, Effingham also saw lucrative possibilities in being governor of Virginia, though his sense of commitment to his duty was sharper than Culpeper's. Together, both men hedged in the Virginians' autonomy but at the cost of making the royal governor the potential enemy of continued self-government.

The General Assembly was established to dispose of routine administrative, legislative, and judicial matters, but it grew into something quite different from what Sir Edwin Sandys, his London Company colleagues, or Charles I had intended. Indeed, the company's dissolution jeopardized its existence. When Charles first commissioned Governor Wyatt, he neglected to instruct him to call the Assembly. The king's oversight had more to do with his ignorance of the Virginia situation than with his animosity toward representative government. No matter the cause, Charles's mistake cast the Assembly into legal limbo. Wyatt, Yeardley, Dr. John Pott, Harvey, and Francis West all set precedent before 1639 when they regularly summoned the Assembly to legislate on such matters as defense and tobacco prices. On their part, Virginians found the Assembly a congenial means of government, as well as a bulwark against a revived company. They aggressively campaigned to "retaine the libertie of our generall Assemblie, then which nothinge can more conduce to our satisfaction or the publique utilitie."[7] Their lobbying bore fruit in 1639, when Governor Wyatt returned to the colony with instructions to call the Assembly annually.

By then, the government's metamorphosis was already afoot. The method for appointing royal councilors was set in 1625, when King Charles included the names of the company incumbents in his commission to Sir Francis Wyatt. From that time until 1776, the crown always named a council at the start of a reign or a new gubernatorial administration. Such changes were not signals for wholesale turnovers in the Council's composition because the crown customarily reconfirmed the incumbents. The governor could, with royal approval, fill vacancies caused by removal, retirement, or death. A place in the Council was for life, unless the holder displeased the king or the governor.

Twelve to sixteen men comprised the full Council during the Jamestown years. Councilors received no salaries, although they and their families were exempted from all taxes and tithes. There were few formal qualifications for the office apart from their being "Gentlemen of the Country."[8] The company had drawn its councilors from England's ruling classes or from those men with experience. That practice continued for some years after 1624, although it was increasingly more common to recruit members from Virginia's emerging society. By mid-century, nearly all of the appointees were long time colonists who had previously served in the House of Burgesses or local government, an indication that past political experience was now viewed as an informal prerequisite for a councillor.

A seat on the Council was also a badge of distinction, for it was the highest political office to which a colonist could rise. It marked an incumbent as someone of superior wealth and ability who had outdone his fellow colonists in the combative world of Virginia politics. To a man, a desire for personal aggrandizement animated the seventeenth-century councilors who saw in land, labor, and family ties the way to political advancement in an expanding society. They arrived in Virginia with advantageous connections or money that gave them a leg up on their less favored fellow settlers. Ambition, skill, and luck drove them to the pinnacle of Virginia society, where they wished to remain. They used the power of their place to grab choice plots of land and tantalizing patronage plums. Marrying into each others' families solidified their control of the levers of powers. Inexorably, these few great conciliar families adopted England's social traditions to a Virginia setting. Their achievements typified the emergence of a native ruling class that in some ways resembled England's.

Changes in the Council's composition accompanied modifications of its responsibilities. Sir Edwin Sandys originally conceived the Council as a body to assist the governor with the colony's management. Such an arrangement seemed possible because the treasurer expected the colonists to build compact settlements close to Jamestown. At the dissolution, the crown inclined toward Sandys's scheme, which explains why it did not alter the Council's membership or its charge. After 1624, however, the idea never worked. Settlements radiated out from the capital in growing numbers as the colony's population swelled. Greater demands on the governor and councilors' time forced the eventual modification of the Council's place in the government of Virginia. Its superintendence of local affairs diminished as its judicial, advisory, and legislative duties enlarged.

Called the "Quarter Court" in its judicial capacity, the Council met quarterly until 1662, when an Act of Assembly reduced the number of sittings to three and changed the name to the "General Court." The governor presided at the sittings, unless he were ill or out of the country, in which case the Council president took the chair. Sessions were limited by law to a maximum of eighteen days "not accompting Sunday in the number," and they were usually timed to coincide with meetings of the Assembly.[9] The councilors tried civil as well as criminal cases, although the adoption of the county form of government in 1634 led to modifications of their jurisdiction. County courts heard all civil actions below a sum fixed by the Assembly. (Their decisions might be appealed to the General Court, and so the councilors assumed the mantle of appellate judges.) All "criminall causes that concerne either life or member" were tried by the councilors before juries, but the adjudication of lesser crimes was also gradually given to the local benches, from which there was no appeal.[10]

General Court litigation bore little resemblance to modern trials. While a trial by jury was accounted "the birthright of every Subject of *England*," a colonist who stood charged with capital offense enjoyed few of the rights that are accorded to today's defendants.[11] Fairness or procedural regularity were alien concepts. Proof of guilt was not held to exacting standards; any testimony was taken as cogent. No lawyer defended the accused, who could not even subpoena witnesses in his behalf. There was no appeal, except for gubernatorial clemency, and that was rarely granted. Trials were swiftly dispatched. Often, the span between the indictment and the execution of the General Court's sentence was a matter of hours, or days at most.

Civil actions were lengthier, more complex, and more numerous. To expedite legal procedure, plaintiffs commenced their suits by filing a document known as a bill which set forth the nature of the action and the desired remedy. Defendants responded with a written answer. The councilors read these records in advance of the trial. On the day of the trial, which could be by jury or not according to the parties' wishes, the General Court took testimony, heard arguments, and made its decision. Cases heard on appeal were retried on their merits instead of being reviewed for procedural irregularities. The court permitted requests for rehearings on all its judgments. As a last resort, its rulings might be appealed to the General Assembly or the king.

Aside from its judicial duties, "the business of the Council," as Robert Beverley explained it, was "to advise the Governor in all Important Matters of Government, and to be a restraint upon him, if he should attempt to exceed the bounds of his Commission: They are enabled to do this, by having each of them an equal Vote with the Governor."[12] Normally, he also deferred to their recommendations about whom to appoint to what offices. The senior councilor in point of service was the Council president, and he was acting governor whenever the chief executive was absent from his post. Claiborne and his colleagues established the precedent for these prerogatives when they ran Governor Harvey off in 1635. Those rights were enlarged during the Berkeley administration because Sir William won his councilors over by giving them "all Places of Trust, Honour, and Profit."[13] Accordingly, the Secretary of the Colony, the Attorney-General, the Auditor-General, the militia commanders, and the various collectors of revenues were always councilors.

With the governor and the burgesses, the councilors constituted the General Assembly. The Assembly convened at the behest of the governor. He issued the call in a proclamation that was read out in the churches, the courts, or any other place that the colonists were likely to gather. In it, he announced the date of the session, the reasons for it, and he commanded the electors to "meete their respective burgesses . . . to present their Agrievances."[14] The proclamation might also include a command for the electors to pick the burgesses.

Elections did not always precede a session because the burgesses did not serve fixed terms, and the idea of rotation in office was still an infant one on both sides of the Atlantic. Moreover, if a governor happened to have a group of burgesses that he found especially congenial, he could extend the life of an Assembly by continually proroguing it, which is what Governor Berkeley did with the so-called Long Assembly that lasted from 1662 to 1676. In such instances, elections were held only when retirement or death caused vacancies. Whatever the reason for the elections, they did not occur until the governor sent authorizing writs to the sheriffs, and to ensure the elections were held, the writs were dispatched well before the date of the Assembly's convening.

In turn, the sheriffs conducted the elections and certified the results. There were no political parties, thus there were no campaigns as we know them. Not all elections were contested because candidates often ran without opposition. No statutory requirements governed who might be a burgess, and theoretically any adult male property owner could stand as a candidate. In practice holding such a major public office was the province of a few prominent county families. Their members viewed the Assembly as their private domain. For much of the century, any free adult male colonist could vote, but the privilege was restricted in 1670 to freeholders, that is, planters who owned or rented at least fifty acres of land. Voters expressed their choices orally, and anyone who failed to vote was liable to a fine. By a 1669 statute, any county that failed to elect two burgesses was subjected itself to stiff penalties.

The elections done, the burgesses and the councilors journeyed to the capital. Travel was slow and the distances between Jamestown and the outlying counties were considerable. Inclement weather added to the difficulties, and everyone avoided the capital in summer or in the midst of the growing season, which was why fall sittings were preferred. Those burgesses and councilors who lived nearest to Jamestown often arrived first. Being closer to town gave them a chance to do a little private business, to politick a bit, or to savor some pints while they waited for the rest of their colleagues.

On the appointed day, the legislators gathered in the statehouse. New members took the oaths of allegiance and supremacy. The burgesses picked the nominee for their speaker and presented him to the governor, together with their request for some of the councilors to assist in their deliberations. Then everyone assembled in the Council chamber to hear the governor deliver his opening speech, which was patterned on the king's speech from the throne at the beginning of Parliament. Like that address, what the governor said was a vital element in the legislative process because it outlined his expectations, and in the hands of clever governors, their speeches ensured results. Then the Assembly got down to the business of perfecting proposed legislation into law. Sessions lasted about three weeks. At the end, the governor signed the newly passed acts, signifying they had now become law, thanked the burgesses for their attendance, and sent them home.

Despite a widely held modern misconception, the General Assembly did not take life as a two-house body possessed of the prerogatives and duties that belong to today's state legislatures or to Congress. It bore only slight resemblance to those bodies for much of the seventeenth century. The powers it possessed by 1700 came not as a consequence of struggles between popularly elected burgesses and royally appointed governors but as the result of rights acquired as the legislators routinely fashioned political or legal solutions to the imperatives of a given moment.

Regular meetings were commonplace well before King Charles authorized them in 1639, and from then until 1677, there was an unbroken string of yearly sessions. (After 1677, later Stuarts discouraged annual sittings as part of their effort to curtail Virginia's independence of their direction.) At first, the governor, the burgesses, and the councilors all met together, a practice they continued until the start of the Berkeley administration. Berkeley arrived in Virginia knowing that the great men among his new constituents thirsted for a share of political power. When he met his first General Assembly in March 1642/43, he encouraged the burgesses to sit separately as the House of Burgesses. He saw the new house as both a means of satisfying aspiring colonial politicians and as a way of garnering support from the other planters. That was but one of many steps in the direction of bicameralism and self-government.

Others that helped to establish the Assembly's legislative prerogatives had been taken years earlier, or they soon followed the House's creation. Early on, taxpayers were charged with paying the burgesses' salaries, as well as with reimbursing their representatives for expenses incurred on public business. As of 1669, when the Assembly passed a law requiring each county to elect "two burgesses for the better service of the publique," it finally made the counties the units of representation and made seats on county benches the prerequisite to House membership.[15] The burgesses had taken control of their house's internal proceedings long before that date. They claimed the sole right to prescribe the credentials for membership as early as 1619 when they refused to seat two of their number whose qualifications were of questionable legality. Then too, they assumed the power to discipline unruly members, and by a statute of March 1623/24, they also freed themselves from arrest "during the time of the assembly, a week before and a week after."[16]

A system of standing committees, chosen by the speaker, came into being around mid-century. Those committees were vital to the orderly dispatch of the House's business, but they were equally important for training the burgesses in legislative procedures. Ultimately, the House fixed its own rules of order. When Berkeley permitted the members of the first House of Burgesses to choose their own speaker and clerk, he laid down a precedent that quickly hardened into a fixed principal which went unchallenged until Governor Effingham's administration. The speaker and the clerk were the House's principal officers. Accordingly, the privilege of picking them without the governor's interference was an important concession to the House's independence.

There were other privileges of equal importance. The Assembly claimed the right to act as a court of last resort. Its claim rested on the London Company's original view of the Assembly as a body vested with administrative, legislative, and judicial duties. After 1619, it regularly took appeals from the General Court until Culpeper and Effingham ware instructed to deny the right as contrary to prevailing English practice.

The burgesses extracted from Governor Wyatt a share of the power to levy and distribute taxes in a statute of March 1623/24. Similarly, from the 1640s onward, the burgesses assumed an increased voice in the initiation of legislation, especially in matters that affected the colony's local government.

Dividing Virginia into counties, as the Assembly did in 1634, seemed an effective way to conclude the search for a workable form of local government. The legislators had grappled with the problem ever since 1619. Their difficulty lay in the failure of Virginia to develop according to expectation. Dispersed settlements made the tasks of local administration troublesome to governor, councilor, and colonist alike. Sharing the responsibility with the proprietors of the particular plantations complicated rather than eased the situation. Governor Wyatt tried to better things when he got a bill creating two monthly courts through the Assembly. The intent was to provide a means of judicial administration and defense in outlying areas, and so the number of these courts soon rose to eight. Their existence only added to a confusion of jurisdictions that overlapped one another. Radical surgery was indicated, and by the 1630s, an adaptation of the English county court appeared to be the prescribed regime. The turn to the county court model marked the start of the Assembly's statutory differentiation between the colony's local and provincial governments, a distinction that was completed in the early 1660s.

Acquiring these and other prerogatives was part and parcel of a larger lawmaking power that the General Assembly arrogated to itself after 1619. At bottom, the making of statutes was the Assembly's raison d'etre. Its laws defined the substance of colonial society, but designing them to fit new circumstances forced the legislators to confront the issue of tailoring English law to an American setting.

The remarkable thing about the refashioning was the background Virginia lawmakers brought to the task. Save for about a dozen, none of the men who sat in the General Assembly between 1619 and 1699 was a lawyer. Few had served in Parliament or held other offices before immigrating to Virginia. Some could barely read or write the vernacular tongue, let alone understand the languages of Latin, English law, and French law. Were those deficiencies a hinderance? Yes and no. The seventeenth-century statutes reveal poor craftsmanship that is certainly attributable to their authors's misapplication of the purpose of laws as well as a fundamental misapprehension of the law of the homeland. Small "wonder if both the Sense of the Law was mistaken, and the Form and Method of the Proceedings was often very irregular," as some colonists were wont to put it.[17] By the same token, lack of experience and formal legal education did not always equal profound ignorance.

The idea of law meant something to every seventeenth-century Englishmen. James Wooley, an obscure contemporary of theirs, spoke for them all when he wrote, "Good is the Law, and to Doe good Designed."[18] Like Wooley, they accepted law — some old, some new, some written, some not, some good, some bad — as the cement of civilized society. They understood how it touched their lives in myriad ways: it distinguished the powerful from the powerless, it terrorized wicked subjects, it preserved good ones, it defined beliefs, and it set them off from other Europeans. Englishmen called their law by the expressive phrase "common law." It was pluralistic and unsystematic, a characteristic which made it unlike the codified civil law of continental nations that derived from Roman precepts. Common law embraced a centuries' old accumulation of custom, precedent, statutes, and judicial decisions that distilled the opinions of innumerable generations regarding the proper ordering of English society.

An awareness of these things in no way depended on one's being trained for a lawyer. Cognizance of them constituted an integral piece of the colonists' intellectual baggage. Colonial lawmakers sprang from mercantile backgrounds that acquainted them with practical aspects of some parts of English law. They could likewise take instruction from the numerous manuals and other legal texts that freely circulated on both sides of the Atlantic.

Their mindset turned them into reformers. They considered the constraints of English society as too confining. That is why these men left home for Virginia with its freer atmosphere in which they might pursue their dreams of aggrandizement by exploiting others. However, even freedom had limits. Without the restraints of law, there could be neither order nor control nor the possibility of fulfillment for the fortunate. Disdainful of old customs and precedents, Virginians lacked the lawyer's instinctive reverence for ancient legal traditions. Their quest for power inclined them to experimentation, and they measured results against a standard of utility. What worked had greater worth than the rigid adherence to antiquated conventions. Results, such as indentured servitude and chattel slavery, could be perversely clever adaptations whose effects have lasted for centuries.

Discovering the workable through lawmaking was reflected in the General Assembly's routine accumulation of legislative rights after 1619. It regulated all manner of human endeavors by the 1670s, and its authority sometimes greatly exceeded that of Parliament. Yet the Assembly was far from omnipotent. Many of its prerogatives rested on no surer foundations than customary usage and the chief executive's sufferance. Its members still defined the public good in terms of the self-interests of their greedy kind, and that tendency created unrest among the planters who were excluded from the circle of privilege. Their disgruntlement led at length to civil war.

Chapter 5
James Cittie in Virginia

John Smith pronounced Jamestown's site "a verie fitt place for the erecting of a great cittie."[1] Company investors, royal officials, governors, and colonists alike shared Smith's optimism throughout the ninety-two years that the colony's capital sat on that spot. However, their calling the place "James Cittie in Virginia," "Jamestown," or simply "the metropolis" bespoke more hope than reality. No city sprang up out of the fort. Jamestown was never anything but a tiny hamlet with few of the attributes of an urban community. Even in its heyday, its several dozen buildings housed a resident population that seldom approached two hundred people. Its failure to develop into Smith's "great cittie" was not for want of effort. Indeed, if persistence alone made cities, then Jamestown should have succeeded, considering how the London Company, the crown, and the colony's own government persisted.

The fort and the town were synonymous during the colony's first years. Situated at the water's edge on the island's western end, the fort encompassed an acre of ground. Its small configuration compelled the residents to live in tight, unsanitary quarters which were a cause of the plague of deadly diseases that cursed the colony. A fire in January 1608 leveled the fort and the buildings that lay in it, but the colonists, with Newport's aid, promptly reconstructed them. During his presidency, Smith oversaw the clearing of more land, the adding of other buildings outside of the fort, and the digging of a well. He left Virginia believing it was in good order, but the trials of the starving time brought the settlement to the edge of extinction. When Sir Thomas Gates arrived from Bermuda in May 1610, he wrote how it "appeared raither as the ruins of some auntient [for]tification, than that any people might now in habit it: the pallisadoes he found tourne downe, the portes open, the gates from the hinges, the church ruined and unfrequented, empty howses . . . rent up and burnt."[2] He would have abandoned Jamestown but for the timely appearance of Governor De la Warr who was prepared "to cleanse the Town" and make another go of it.[3]

Slowly, the "cleansing" got results, especially during the years that Gates and Sir Thomas Dale were in charge. They vigorously enforced provisions in *The Lawes Divine, Morall and Martiall* that forbade throwing wash water "in the open street" or "renching" utensils near the well, just as they punished anyone who "within lesse then a quarter of one mile from the Pallizadoes, [dared] to doe the necessities of nature."[4] They also "reduced [Jamestown] into a hansome forme." At least that is how Ralph Hamor described the town's look in 1614. He went on to say "it hath in it two faire rowes of howses, all of framed Timber,

A fire in 1608 leveled the fort and the buildings that lay in it.

Jamestown circa 1614 to 1619.

two stories high, and an upper Garret, or Corne loft high, besides three large, and substantiall Storehowses, joined togeather in length some hundred and twenty foot, and in breadth forty, and this town hath been lately newly, and strongly impaled."[5]

Some additional farm houses and cleared fields, he noted, lay to the north and east of the pale, while strategically placed block houses guarded against attack from the mainland.

Hamor's depiction revealed that Jamestown had at last assumed a recognizable shape, and that was of a village modeled roughly to the pattern of an Ulster plantation. Such plantations, which were instrumental in the conquest of Ireland, consisted of a stoutly armed bastion, or "castle," and a palisaded courtyard the English called a "bawn." Experienced soldiers such as Gates and Dale were quite well-acquainted with their countrymen's Irish ventures. Warring and colonizing in Ireland had been commonplace up to Jamestown's founding; both continued long after 1607. Settlers who colonized the Emerald Isle taught Virginia's backers much about survival in hostile territory that had application in the New World. Not the least of these lessons was the value of fortified villages and how to plan them. Moreover, the Ulster design helped to reinforce the military organization the London Company tried to impose on Virginia during the years between the charter revisions of 1609 and 1618.

Notwithstanding the effort, Jamestown did not prosper as expected. Discipline slackened when *The Lawes Divine, Morall and Martiall* fell into disuse following Dale's departure for England in 1616. As other settlements sprang up all along the length of the James from its mouth to its falls, they siphoned off planters who were drawn to more healthful sites. Of course, no one thought to abandon Jamestown. It remained Virginia's principal settlement and administrative center, even though its population dwindled to a mere fifty men, plus some women and children by 1616. Rolfe's experiments with tobacco also retarded Jamestown's continued growth. No sooner had Rolfe succeeded than every other colonist sought to emulate him; they forsook everything else and "dispersed all about, planting *Tobacco*," leaving buildings and pallisades about the town to decay.[6]

When Deputy-Governor Samuel Argall landed at Jamestown in 1617, he found the entire place in a dilapidated condition. He restored things "agreeable to his owne minde," including the construction of a frame church that stood until the 1630s. His insistence on the repairs "did exceedingly trouble" the colonists, who resented being compelled to leave their tobacco fields to fix the town. Nevertheless, Argall's renovations anticipated an expansion of Jamestown that followed in the wake of Sir Edwin Sandys's reforms of the Virginia operation.[7]

Sandys employed William Claiborne as a surveyor and sent him to Virginia in 1621 with Governor Wyatt. Ostensibly, Claiborne's task was to plot accurate boundaries for the fast-growing number of land grants that Sandys used as lures to attract colonists. Claiborne, who parlayed this opportunity into a lucrative political career, also surveyed a "new towne" to accommodate the colony's expected growth. For the site, he selected a tract of ground that lay downriver about half a mile east of the fort, which he laid off in gridiron fashion. Although no copy of Claiborne's scheme survives, the layout may be surmised from descriptions found in some of the lot surveys. Accordingly, the gridiron extended for about a thousand feet along an east-west line. On one side ran "the high way close to the bank of the Maine River." This highway linked up with the "Greate Road" that passed near the older settlement on its route across the isthmus to the mainland. A "Backe Streete" paralleled the river road, while both thoroughfares were joined by two or three shorter streets that intersected them at right angles.

The massacre and the ensuing war temporarily disrupted New Town's development. The settlers momentarily considered abandoning Jamestown in favor of a stronghold on the Eastern Shore, but the company scotched that idea. Once the danger of attack subsided, New Town prospered, especially during the latter half of the 1620s when some of Virginia's more important inhabitants acquired lots and built on them. Sir John Harvey patented a large property in 1624 that was situated between Backe Streete and the river road in the development's eastern extremity. He constructed several dwellings on it, including a two-unit residence, and he maintained gardens and orchards as well. To the west of his land were lots belonging to George Menifie, a merchant and councilor; John Chew, another merchant; Ralph Hamor, Sir Thomas Dale's Secretary of the Colony; and Richard Stephens, who frequently quarreled with Harvey. Dr. John Pott, the sometime acting governor who employed his knowledge of medicine to poison Indians, was among those living along Backe Streete, or north of it. Others included Governor Wyatt, Edward Blaney, William Pierce, and Roger Smith, each of whom sat in the General Assembly.

New Town's effect on the old quarter is far from certain, though it may be guessed with some assurance. Argall's church remained as a focus of religious and social activity. The wooden fort rotted and tumbled apart. At some point it was probably replaced by an earthen bastion that mounted several cannon. Once the English seated the "subberbs" on the north mainland, the danger of Indian attack receded, and there was no longer any need for the palisade. The blockhouses fell into disuse. Inhabitants fanned out along the ridges that rimmed the Pitch and Tar

Swamp well before the disappearance of the fence's remaining vestiges. One of these was the Rev. Thomas Hampton, who lived on glebe land that the Assembly provided to the town rector. Most of the high ground on the island's eastern end was woods or farmland.

Establishing New Town had no immediate effect on the transformation of Jamestown into a viable community. When Harvey took up the government in 1630, the capital was without any taverns or inns, and it was still without any public buildings. The Assembly continued to meet in the church "quire," while sessions of the Quarter Court or the Council probably convened either at the governor's house or else in one of the councilors' homes. Harvey intimated as much when he wrote to England complaining that his residence was a "randezvous for all sorts of strangers" and "a generall harbour for all comers."[8]

Always the determined man, Harvey aimed to rectify these indignities. He managed several pieces of legislation through the General Assembly, in spite of his difficulties with the Council. One was a statute of February 1631/32 making Jamestown Virginia's sole port of entry. By confining the tobacco trade to the capital, the hope was that the town's growth would match that of the colony. Another required skilled craftsmen to work at their trades and not "to plant tobacco or corne or doe any other worke in the ground," while a 1633 act gave Jamestown's storekeeper custody of the colony's official "sealed weights" and "true stilliards [i.e., steelyards]"[9] A law passed in 1636 promised a house lot and garden plot to anyone who settled at Jamestown and built a house within six months.

The results appeared to bear out Harvey's determination and the king's instructions. In 1638, Sir John optimistically reported to his superiors in London that there were now

> twelve houses and stores built in the Towne, one of brick by the Secretarye [i.e., Richard Kemp], the fairest that ever was knowen in this countrye for substance and uniformitye, by whose example others have undertaken to build framed howses to beautifye the place, consonant to his majesties Instruction that wee should not suffer men to build slight cottages as heretofore.

Furthermore, he wrote, "a levye . . . is raised for the building of a State howse."[10]

The "State howse" was never built according to Harvey's plan. The Assembly evidently used the "levye" to buy Harvey's house which the ex-governor sold to the colony in 1641. It was then converted into Virginia's first statehouse.

When Berkeley was appointed, his instructions indicated that the crown thought Harvey's optimism was somewhat misplaced. King Charles I commanded the new governor to raise towns by requiring every land owner whose holdings exceeded five hundred acres to erect brick dwellings at Jamestown or some other location. Moreover, because "the Buildings at James Town are for the most part decayed, and the place found to be unhealthy," Berkeley's instructions also authorized him "to choose such other Seate for the Chiefe Town" as he saw fit, and it would retain "the Ancient name of James Town."[11] Intent on winning Virginia's great men, Berkeley never attempted to relocate the capital; for the same reason he was equally reluctant to propose implementing the other part of Charles's instructions.

Instead, he committed himself to developing Jamestown into a thriving community. Leading by example, he thought, was the likeliest way to obtain results. However, the example he set was not exactly what the crown might have wished. He started his own brick three-unit rowhouse in town, but he also began work on his country plantation, Green Spring. In time, Green Spring, not the townhouse, became the object of the great planters' emulation.

The Indian War of 1644-1646 and Virginia's growth threw a crimp into Sir William's plans for Jamestown. Opechancanough's unexpected attack, once it was contained, sent Berkeley on a hurried trip back to England to purchase much-needed arms and ammunition. With a war on, few of the great men chanced their energies or treasure on townhouses in the capital. While the construction work on both of Berkeley's residences slowed, it never ceased altogether. As Secretary Kemp reported in a letter he sent the governor in February 1644/45, "your people are all in good health and safetie att the Greene Springe and the brickehouse there is now in hand, but that att towne for want of materialls is yet no higher than the first storye above the Cellar."[12]

Opechancanough's war impeded the colonists' expansion, but only for a little while. Civil war in England drove thousands of new colonists to Virginia, many of whom flocked to seat the territory north and west of the York River basin. Some had already carved out plantations along the Potomac even as the 1640s drew to their end, but not that many immigrants saw opportunity in Jamestown and town living. Most of the newer colonists generally avoided James Cittie as a place to make their fortunes. Still, the exertions of Berkeley and others on the town's behalf had wrought noticeable changes before Sir William surrendered Virginia to Puritan control in the spring of 1652. By then its capital had acquired some of the characteristics of a stable community.

The town docks bustled as vessels called from New England, the West Indies, or Europe and left with holds gorged with tobacco. They linked Jamestonians to the Atlantic water highway that made England seem somehow less remote than Virginia's frontier fringes. Berkeley's rowhouse and the statehouse symbolized the town's importance to colonial

Brick house at Jamestown about 1650.

The "Long House" residential complex.

75

politics, as well as the political ties to the mother country. There was the jail, which held prisoners who awaited trial at the Quarter Court, and where Opechancanough was incarcerated before his murder in 1644.

A substantial brick church dominated the landscape. Begun in 1639 and completed by 1644, the new church took its architectural inspiration from English country churches of the period. Although it was slightly larger than its predecessor, it was of moderate scale, but its three-foot thick walls gave it a feeling of solidity and permanence. Construction of a three-story tower was completed around 1647, and its addition easily made the church Jamestown's most impressive landmark. That visual impression mainly served to reinforce the church as a focus of life at Jamestown. It solaced the godly who sought spiritual comfort in the rituals of the Church of England. On Sundays or other holy days, the priest customarily read out gubernatorial proclamations, election writs, matrimonial banns, or other notices. Last, and certainly not least, the church provided a regular meeting place where parishioners might tarry to talk of the weather or to trade gossip.

The area around New Town had the flavor of a residential quarter. From the beginning, it was the neighborhood of choice, and it continued as a distinct section of Jamestown for more than twenty years after Claiborne laid it out. The distinction blurred as more residents settled north of Backe Streete and west of the old Harvey tract. New Town finally lost its identity in the early 1650s when it was no longer distinguishable from the rest of the metropolis.

Houses of varying size and construction bespoke their owners' differing degrees of wealth and standing. Tradesmen's houses were easy to pick out from the others. They doubled as places of business, and so their design was more functional than stylish. Rude thatched cottages made of plaster and laths, or "wattle-and-daub," as the English called the technique, sheltered the poorer residents or the recent arrivals. Sturdier frame dwellings were the most common house type to be seen about Jamestown. (There were no log cabins, as that was a form of housing as yet undiscovered by the English.) A number of brick homes dotted the townscape. Several of these were rowhouses; the rest were single-family structures. No matter who built them, all of Jamestown's houses would seem primitive by modern standards. Small of dimension and short on refinement, they afforded their occupants little privacy or comfort.

Jamestown mirrored Virginia's society in certain respects. The residents were mostly young males, which meant that any increase in the number of inhabitants was due more to immigration than to natural addition. About half of the townspeople worked as indentured servants. A tiny, but highly visible contingent of black Africans foretold a none-too-distant day when slavery would be the colony's predominant

In 1619, a cargo of twenty Africans were sold in Virginia.

labor system. Bondsmen who survived the rigors of servitude to become propertyless freemen eked out a minimal existence as day laborers or petty thieves. The more substantial citizens mixed commerce, trade, and farming in their quest for wealth and position. These gradations evidenced an emerging social order of unequals in which the few profited from the labors of the many.

Despite the difficulty with keeping craftsmen at their trades, Jamestown drew a disproportionate share of potters, brewers, masons, brickmakers, limeburners, coopers, smiths, boatwrights, carpenters, sawyers, and assorted others, all of whom managed to flourish in their traditional occupations. Brewers especially found the capital a congenial place in which to ply their trade because, according to one observer, "Six publike Brewhouses" were in existence as of 1649.[13] Although brewmasters and the other skilled artisans conducted their businesses at various locations, their tendency was to concentrate in what, without undue exaggeration, might be denominated "industrial zones." One of these lay on the river bank to the east of the church. A warehouse, a brick kiln, a lime kiln, and either a bakery or brewery, plus some sort of forge, all sat there. The other zone rimmed the Pitch and Tar Swamp, and it comprised a pottery kiln, a smelting pit, another brick kiln, and a brewery.

The erection of breweries testifies to the existence of taverns in the town. All of them were regulated by the Assembly, which is why they were commonly called ordinaries. Some antedated 1640, the year the Assembly began setting the prices of liquor, lodgings, and food. In the mid-1640's the Assembly attempted to limit the growth of ordinaries by restricting the "retayle" of "wine or strong waters" to established public houses.[14] Their presence added an amenity that Jamestown had formerly lacked, and it relieved Sir John Harvey's successors of having to provide a "generall harbour" for visitors.

Another amenity was the creation in 1649 of a new, expanded public market. The original market sat on land that once lay inside the old palisade. That site lost its appeal in the 1640s. It was close to the area that was being converted into industrial zones, it lacked space sufficient to meet the needs of the vendors, and it was inconvenient to people who lived in the New Town area. Consequently, the Assembly set off a substantial tract downriver from the old Harvey property for a weekly market. Bounded by the Back River, "Sandy Gutt," and "the gutt next beyond the house of Lancelott Elay" respectively, the new market was intended to duplicate the activities of an English market town. It stayed open on Wednesdays and Saturdays from morning until evening. A "clerke of the markett," whom Berkeley appointed, presided over its activities. He kept the offical weights and measures and he also attested

Farm scene and Virginia produce circa 1650.

78

to the validity of all sales made within the market's precincts.[15]

Promising as these developments were, they did not prompt Jamestown's continued expansion because the times were not propitious during the Interregnum. With Berkeley out of power, there was no one to push for more growth. He sold off part of his townhouse and spent his forced retirement improving Green Spring. Others, who shared the ex-governor's strong royalist sympathies, also abandoned the town for the country. Parliament's initial stab at regulating colonial trade, the Navigation Act of 1651, and the First Anglo-Dutch War constricted Virginia's economy. The Assembly had other interests. Virginia's Commonwealth governors, who were not venturesome spirits, showed little inclination to goad it in the town's favor. To a man, they were also hampered by their unpopularity as the representatives of an alien Puritan authority.

After the first statehouse burned in 1655, the Assembly elected not to rebuild it immediately. Instead, the members reverted to the old habit of using private residences as meeting places. They finally settled on a permanent location in 1657. It was a large brick house that stood by pitch and tar, north and west of the old capitol site. A fire consumed it in 1660, but it was not replaced at once. For the moment, this loss was diminished by King Charles II's restoration and Governor Berkeley's return to power.

When Berkeley resumed his post, he envisioned the revitalization of his capital as part of an ambitious scheme to reshape Virginia's economy. He got the Assembly's authorization "to take into his care the building of a state-house."[16] Then he sailed to England, where he sought royal sanction for his plans. Renewing his instructions to Berkeley, Charles II ordered that

> there may be at least one Town upon every River and that you begin at James River, which being first seated we desire to give all countenance and settle the Govvernment there, and therefore as we do expect that you will give good example yourself by building some houses, those which will in short time turn to your profit, so you shall in our name let the Councellors of that Colony know that we will take it very well if they will each of them build one or more houses there.[17]

No sooner had Berkeley returned to Jamestown than he issued writs for the election of a new General Assembly from which he got the necessary legislation in December 1662.

In what could be called America's first flirtation with urban renewal, the "act for building a town" called for the construction of thirty-two new brick houses in Jamestown. Each was to be roofed with slate or pantiles, which would lessen the danger of fire. All were to be raised "one

King Charles II

by another in a square or such other forme as the honorable Sir William Berkeley shall appoint most convenient." Seventeen of them were to be built at taxpayers' expense by the county courts. The remainder were the responsibility of private "undertakers." To attract such developers, the act provided for certain monopolies and subsidies. The latter came from a special colony-wide poll tax of 30 lbs. of tobacco per capita. Finally, the statute prohibited the repair or erection of any wooden houses within Jamestown's corporate "limitts."[18]

The results did not match expectations. Berkeley proved a poor town planner. He permitted builders to locate haphazardly about Jamestown, just as he failed to insist that they fabricate single-family dwellings. Consequently, some of the new construction was in the form of row-housing. Then too, he dallied for more than five years before he started his promised reconstruction of the statehouse. Such indolence was hardly the sort of leadership King Charles expected of his governor. And yet, in 1665, as Secretary Thomas Ludwell noted, there were enough new houses to accommodate the "publique affairs of the country."[19] Although he gave no indication of how many of these structures there were, the number never approached what the town law envisioned. Ten years later, only twelve were in existence, and most of them were used as ordinaries.

Berkeley's shortcomings as a builder of cities are not the whole reason for Jamestown's incomplete rehabilitation. Apart from Secretary Ludwell and Lt. Gov. Francis Moryson, few of the councilors jumped at the opportunity to become real estate promoters. Berkeley reported their resistance to London, acidly observing that they still "looked back on England with hopes that the selling of what they have here will make them live plentifully there."[20] Without their example, the less well-to-do planters felt little compulsion to participate in the redevelopment of the capital. The rush of enthusiasm spent itself as the 1660s yielded to a new decade and the colonists turned their attentions elsewhere. Renewal ran its course about the time a young colonist named Nathaniel Bacon first saw "James Cittie in Virginia."

Chapter 6

Civil War

Bacon's Rebellion burst across the Old Dominion in the spring of 1676 against a backdrop of hard times and terrifying Indian raids. Angered at Governor Berkeley's apparent unwillingness to protect them, disaffected colonists cast their lot with a young newcomer, who eagerly made their cause his own. In so doing, Nathaniel Bacon plunged Virginia into civil war. Jamestown figured prominently in the revolt; indeed, the consequences for the capital were disastrous.

For ordinary Virginians, hard times started with the restoration of King Charles II in 1660. The king, his brother, James, Duke of York, and their underlings came back to England determined to mold Virginia to their conceptions of empire. They presupposed an imperial system grounded in social order, political obedience, military security, and the exclusion of the Dutch from the Virginia trade. Achieving the vision meant limiting the Old Dominion's independence. Parliament created one such limitation when it enacted into law a system of trade regulations known as the navigation acts. Virginians, especially those with ties to Dutch merchants, decried the trade laws' strictures on their access to foreign markets.

Governor Berkeley opposed the navigation acts. He went to London in 1661 to work against them, but he failed. Resolutely, he returned to his government the next year bent on transforming Virginia according to his own scheme for its place in a larger English empire. He foresaw Virginia's prosperity arising from integrated settlements, a diversified economy, and a hierarchical society where men could foster their personal ambitions without much interference from the crown. Such a colony, he thought, would redound to England's greater benefit than would the strictly regulated imperium Charles II now favored.

What Berkeley wanted was predicated on his persuading Virginia's planters to curtail tobacco production and to diversify the colony's economy, as he obtained a financial commitment from the crown to underwrite some of the experiments with cash crops other than tobacco. English officials at first inclined toward encouraging Berkeley, although they gave nothing out of the royal coffers. But once they recognized that diversification meant smaller tobacco crops, and smaller tobacco crops meant less income from the tobacco duties, they withheld their support. Berkeley had no trouble pushing the enabling legislation past a pliant General Assembly, but he never cajoled more than a few planters to diversify, and by 1669 he gave up trying. Then too, he was unsuccessful in his efforts to persuade the governments of Maryland and Carolina to join Virginia in a general reduction of tobacco crops. His failures cost him politically, while the planters paid heavily in increased taxes.

From the point of view of ordinary Virginians, Stuart colonial policy and their governor's schemes were misbegotten. They faced a threatening economic situation brought on by the overproduction of tobacco that kept their prices low and their debts high. The navigation laws compelled them to sell their tobacco only in England which saturated the market with surpluses and drove its price down to the point where their crops would "not cloath them and their Families."[1] Diversification raised their taxes that escalated with the mounting costs of county government. Pinched by low prices and high taxes, the planters turned hostile toward the men who controlled the county courts.

A small group of men, about 375 in number, had come to control all local offices by 1676. Moreover, they also succeeded in turning the counties into the basis for representation in the House of Burgesses and making a seat on the bench an opening for the General Assembly or the Council of State. At the same time the justices plotted these lines of political authority, they also set the foundations for a native ruling class. Officeholding became the symbol of one's exalted standing for it signified that a justice had surpassed his less-successful neighbors in the quest for riches and preferment. Having attained the coveted prize, he intended to pass it on through his kin connections or political alliances with other justices.

The group's domination was virtually complete in 1668, when the General Assembly stopped creating new counties, and the number of additional county offices diminished. Closing this route to advancement magnified the rivalry for the available slots. Besides that, county magnates lacked the approbation of their fellow colonists. They stood at the head of Virginia society not because of an immemorial tradition, but only because they had beat the others to the top spot. Such men saw their offices more as places of private gain than of public trust and they frequently misused their great power, which was itself as yet not well-defined. Their insensitivity to those beneath them and their own insecurity made the politics of the 1660s and 1670s brutish in both tone and substance.

Nasty politics heightened free Virginians' fears of indentured servants, slaves, and ex-bondsmen. Predominantly male, youthful, and ungovernable, bound laborers constituted more than half of the Old Dominion's inhabitants. These individuals, who suffered from overwork and mistreatment, ran off, stole, or resisted their masters at any opportunity, while former laborers made up a sizeable underclass that existed by preying on other settlers. What was frightful to "respectable" colonists was the possibility that the two groups might combine to revolt against their condition, something which almost happened on at least one occasion before 1676.

An even greater fear lay in the likelihood that the colonists might one day confront the horrifying prospect of simultaneously defending against rebellious servants, the Indians, and some foreign invader. Nominally, peace had existed with the remnants of the old Powhatan coalition since the conclusion of the last war in 1646, but there were enduring animosities that by the 1660s led to isolated, but not infrequent, skirmishes along the frontier. These episodes might have given way to renewed warfare but for Berkeley's swift actions to stay it. Charles II's closure of Virginia to Dutch traders helped spark the Second and Third Anglo-Dutch Wars. Berkeley, who knew only too well Virginia's vulnerability to Dutch attacks, begged the home government for cannon, gunpowder, and other military hardware to prepare adequate defenses, but to little result. Royal officials compelled Sir William to abandon his own plans, which included the costly renovation of the fort at Jamestown, in favor of expensive fortifications at the mouth of the James River. He and every other Virginian knew such emplacements would be useless because no cannon could shoot across the river's width. Events proved him right. In 1667, and again in 1673, Dutch privateers sailed into the Chesapeake Bay without warning and burned the tobacco fleets as they lay at anchor.

The last of these raids widened a breech between the governor and the planters, for it demonstrated the bankruptcy of Berkeley's defensive planning. Added taxes for arms and forts failed to fend off the Dutch. Berkeley became the object of loud complaints that boiled over in the fall of 1673, when the Assembly again hiked the levies to re-equip all the local militias. Ratepayers in several counties balked at the new assessments, even to the point of trying to prevent the higher assessments from being collected. These outbursts should have been a caution to Berkeley. They were not. Instead, he saw them as no more than the posturing of a few extremists, whom he eventually pardoned. The real troublemakers, the venal county politicians and some in Berkeley's own circle, went unpunished. His want of discernment showed that old age had dulled his faculties at the very moment his ability to govern was being doubted as never before.

As he aged into his late sixties, Berkeley, a man noted for his tart personality, grew more acerbic, which heightened his subordinates' difficulties in dealing with him. When trusted friends or confidants who held provincial offices died, he filled the vacancies with the colony's younger politicians and recent immigrants. Increasingly, Berkeley sought only the advice of his surviving friends such as Philip and Thomas Ludwell, Robert Beverley, or that of his second wife, Frances Culpeper

Stephens, Lady Berkeley, whom he wed in 1670.* These individuals' hold over him was itself a cause of discontent within the inner circle, as everyone angled for the most promising spot against the day when the old man either died or tumbled into royal disfavor. As for Berkeley, he displayed no ability, or desire, to stay the infighting. Only luck spared him down to the mid-1670s. However much the planters and the big men may have wished him dead or out of power, there was no one who dared to capitalize on the discontent by challenging his leadership. Berkeley's luck turned in 1675.

On "a Sabbath day Morning in the summer Anno 1675, People in their Way to Church," discovered that Doeg Indians had just attacked a plantation up in Stafford County, where they stole some hogs, killed an overseer, and then slipped back into Maryland.[2] On its face, the raid was similar to incidents that were commonplace along the frontier's edges, and when the Stafford militia commanders heard the news, they knew what to do. They called up a troop of militiamen, marched into Maryland, and slaughtered a few Doegs. Unfortunately, the troopers also murdered some innocent Susquehannocks, whose countrymen swiftly avenged their loss with a series of lethal strikes all along the Virginia-Maryland frontier.

Word of all this slowly made its long way from Stafford to Jamestown. When Governor Berkeley at last heard about the latest troubles, he had difficulty separating truth from fiction. The intelligence alarmed him, but he withheld action until he was better advised as to what he should do. He hurriedly called the Council of State into session. They counseled him to order an investigation by local magistrates and a retaliatory strike, "as shall be found necessary and Just."[3] Berkeley took the advice, and on August 31, he issued the necessary orders to two Westmoreland

---

* Although it is not generally known, Frances Culpeper Stephens was not Governor Berkeley's first wife. Berkeley, it seems, married for the first time about the year 1650. Details of the marriage are sketchy; all that is certain is that it took place. Its existence is established by two independent sources. One was Virginia Ferrar, who was the sister of an investor in the London Company, Nicholas Ferrar of Little Giddings. The other was John, Lord Berkeley, the governor's elder brother. Virginia Ferrar wrote a letter to mysterious Lady Berkeley on 10 Aug. 1650, in which she refers to the lady as "the Noble Governors happy Consorte." Another letter, undated and addressed to an anonymous kinsman of Madame Ferrar, also mentions the marriage as having occurred shortly before Virginia Ferrar wrote it, but it affords no illumination as to the identity of Lady Berkeley. (See Ferrar Papers, Magdalene College, Cambridge University, Oxford.) In a letter that John, Lord Berkeley wrote to Edward Hyde — later the Earl of Clarendon — on 25 Sept. 1650, he mentioned that "Will Berkeley is married," though he furnished no further details about the marriage. (See Clarendon Papers, Bodleian Library, Oxford University.) Indeed, the offhandedness of the remark suggests that Lord Berkeley did not view the wedding as unexpected.

Frontiersmen and their settlements felt the fullness of the Indians' wrath.

County justices of the peace, John Washington and Isaac Allerton.

Bent on revenge, Allerton and Washington failed to follow their orders precisely. They quickly collected a troop of men and asked the governor of Maryland for assistance in tracking down the marauding Susquehannocks. The Marylanders complied by calling up some of their militia, and when they linked up with the Virginians, the combined force set out to locate the Indians. Some weeks later, they discovered their enemy's stronghold on the Maryland side of the Potomac. The Susquehannocks at first inclined to negotiate, but that inclination evaporated after the English perfidiously executed five of their chiefs during a truce. Having no artillery to bombard it, the English lay siege to the fort. Their siege came to a sudden end one night some weeks later when the Susquehannocks used the cover of darkness to escape into the forest. Enraged at this unexpected turn of events, the frustrated colonists could only curse their stupidity as they marched home with the knowledge that their expedition had failed miserably.

Thereafter, the frontiersmen felt the fullness of the natives' wrath as the Susquenhannocks attacked settlements across the fall line. The deadliest of their attacks came in January 1676, when thirty-six colonists died in a single raid. At that point, the Susquehannocks concluded that they had balanced the account for the loss of their slain chiefs, whereupon they made known their desire for a truce. Berkeley would not negotiate, and so they retreated westward into the interior, well beyond the remotest English settlement.

The Susquehannocks' withdrawal did not put a stop to the carnage. Other natives took advantage of the colonists' distress to avenge wrongs the English had done them through the years. The identity of these Indians was a matter of sharp controversy at the time, but the result of what they did was indisputable. Unlike the Susquehannocks, who were satiated with killing Englishmen and taking food or livestock, these Indians systematically looted and burned every settlement they hit. Convinced that the long-feared alliance of the Indians was at hand the terrified planters begged their governor for help.

Berkeley promptly answered the call. He ordered the lieutenant governor, Sir Henry Chicheley, to muster 300 men and head for the frontier to fight any Indians he might engage. Sir Henry spent little time in collecting the men, but his troop never marched because Berkeley quite unexpectedly changed his mind. He sent the men home, saying that he intended to call the General Assembly into session and lay the whole Indian business before it. The decision confounded everyone, not only because of its untimeliness but because the governor would not explain the reasons for it. Worse still, he was oblivious to the political implications of leaving unprotected colonists defenseless. He seemed to them an indecisive old man who lacked the stomach for a fight.

Wild rumors and tales of new assaults greeted the members of the Asscmbly who hastened to Jamestown for the opening of the session on March 28, 1676. The tensions of the moment tautened everyone's nerves to the snapping point. There was no forecasting what either the Indians or the governor might do next. As much as they feared the "insulting enimmies" not one of the legislators wished openly to criticize Berkeley because he frightened them too. Besides, there was still a chance that he might carry the colony through to better times, and they would then look foolish for opposing him. Expediency dictated that they follow his lead, at least for the time being.

The Assembly acted favorably on Berkeley's recommendations to mount a defensive war and to leave command decisions to him. His plan was basically the same as one he had devised thirty years earlier when he fought Opechancanough to a standstill. Accordingly, the Assembly enacted a bill to raise a garrison of 500 men. Some of them were to construct and man nine forts established at the heads of the rivers and other strategic locations. The rest were to range between the forts in search of the natives. However, the law prohibited their commanders from attacking enemy raiders "untill order shall come from the governour."[4] To pay for the scheme, the Assembly voted new taxes.

Nothing about the plan soothed panic-stricken colonists or dispelled doubts about Berkeley. Planters all across Virginia condemned the scheme, arguing that stationary fortifications had little value against a mobile enemy who attacked without warning. Repeatedly, the frontier petitioned Berkeley, pleading "that your gratious Honor would be pleased to grant us a Commition and to make choice of Commitioned officers" who would protect them.[5] Berkeley coldly turned such pleas aside, and he even refused to countenance additional petitions on the subject.

In April, a rumor made the circuit in Charles City County to the effect that several contingents of hostile Indians lay within striking distance of the county's borders south of the James. The news incited the residents, who "beat up the drum for Volunteers to goe out against the Indians" and dispatched emisaries to Jamestown to demand someone for a leader, but Berkeley would have none of that.[6] This time, however, the angry petitioners were not to be denied. Once they got back to their homes, they and other like-minded planters armed themselves and started to look for a commander. They found him in the person of Nathaniel Bacon.

Bacon's enthusiasm for their enterprise derived from a chance conversation with three of his friends, Henry Isham, James Crews, and William Byrd I. Bacon and his friends were no ordinary upcountry colonists. Isham was a wealthy Charles City County planter with ties to some of the county's reputable families. Byrd and Crews sat on the Henrico County Court and held commissions in the local militia. Although Bacon was comparatively new to colonial politics, he was one of Berkeley's councilors as well as a relation. The four were greatly alarmed by the Indian troubles, especially Bacon and Byrd, both of whom had lost servants and property to the most recent raids. All four believed that the governor was too old and too feeble to prevent further attacks, let alone teach the natives a proper lesson. The plans he got through the late Assembly seemed to confirm their suspicions, just as his concern for protecting the tributary tribes heightened their feeling that he cared more for the Indian trade, which he controlled, than for the lives of Englishmen.

Their talk continued in that vein until someone spoke of hearing how a group of Southsiders was unwilling to depend on Berkeley any longer. These individuals, so the story went, had armed themselves and encamped on the south bank of the James near Jordan's Point. The four discussed the merits of such direct action a while longer before they decided to visit the campground to see what was going on. No sooner had they arrived than the volunteers greeted them with shouts of "A Bacon! A Bacon! A Bacon!" as they entreated the councilor to lead them. And he obliged.

Who was Nathaniel Bacon? The plain truth is, no one knows. His contemporaries could not agree on his character or his motives. To his enemies, he was "young, bold, active, of an inviting Aspect, and powerful Elocution. In a word, he was every way qualified to head a giddy and unthinking Multitude."[7] To his followers, he was "our hopes of safety; liberty, our all."[8] To this day, scholars are just as divided in their opinions because they have so few details from which to fashion an accurate assessment of Bacon.

This much is certain. Nathaniel Bacon was born in 1647 into the family of Sir Thomas Bacon of Friston Hall in Suffolk. Squire Bacon reared his son in a manner that befit the English gentry. The boy attained a smattering of both a university and legal education before he made the grand tour of Europe. Young Bacon married Elizabeth Duke in 1670, against the wishes of her father, who disinherited her. Now a man with a family, Bacon tried unsuccessfully to establish himself. His involvement in some fraudulent dealings caused an exasperated Sir Thomas to ship the pair off to Virginia, where they might prosper under the watchful eyes of his cousins, Councilor Nathaniel Bacon, Sr. and Governor Berkeley. Shortly after Nathaniel and Elizabeth Bacon landed in Virginia in 1674, the couple purchased a working plantation whose main tract lay forty miles by water above Jamestown in Henrico County on the James at a site called "Curles Neck." Berkeley named his young kinsman to a vacancy on the Council of State less than six months after his arrival. Few Virginians of the day had ever risen so high so fast. Bacon showed little interest in his conciliar duties, but his seat on the Council marked him as a man of "great Honour and Esteem among the People."[9] By the time of the Indian troubles he had attracted a following of notable men about him.

Three of them were his neighbors and close friends, Byrd, Crews, and Isham. They, like Bacon, wanted a share of the Indian trade, even though they detested the natives; in business, profits mattered more than personal dislikes. Richard Lawrence, Giles Bland, William Drummond, and William Carver completed the circle of intimates. A sometime Oxford scholar, Lawrence lived at Jamestown where he kept a tavern and occasionally represented Lower Norfolk County in the House of Burgesses. Bland held a royal commission as customs collector, a post that led him into frequent trouble with the governor, whom he despised. Drummond was a Scot, who had a long-standing feud with Berkeley over some land grants in the Albemarle country and his proper compensation for rebuilding the fort at Jamestown. Carver, who was once a mariner before he settled in Lower Norfolk County, was a justice of the peace and a member of the General Assembly until he lost the seat in 1671. The other followers numbered men like Thomas Hansford, Thomas Cheesman, Joseph Ingram, and Gregory Walklett, who were either from respectable but modest families or recent immigrants who had settled on the frontier.

Being in such company exhilarated Bacon, especially after his visit to the volunteers' camp at Jordan's Point. At that moment, he perhaps believed his office and kinship with the governor were such that his cousin would permit him to lead the angry planters against their mortal enemy. He was wrong. Accepting command of these unauthorized voluteers was contrary to law, and Sir William was not a man to countenance an act which was both tantamount to mutiny and an affront to his authority.

Nevertheless, Berkeley had no wish to combat a mutiny in the midst of his other difficulties. On hearing that his relative had taken command of the volunteers, he dispatched a messenger with a note warning Bacon not to proceed and ordering him to the capital for a meeting. Bacon disregarded the caution, though he asked Berkeley for a legal commission even as he continued to prepare for his campaign. Infuriated at Bacon's refusal to abide by his commands, Berkeley impulsively marshalled some militia and hastened to cut Bacon off before he marched into the interior. By the time he reached Henrico, Bacon had decamped, and the governor looked the fool for his efforts.

From that moment on, the quarrel between the two men took on a sharper edge. No sooner had the weary, befuddled Berkeley returned to Jamestown on May 10 than he issued an angry proclamation dismissing Bacon from the Council of State and declaring him a rebel. That same day, he published two other pronouncements aimed at undercutting Bacon's growing popularity. One was a call for a new General Assembly "for the redress of all such Greviances of the Country may justly complaine of and for the better security of the Country from our Barbarous Enemies the Indians and better settling and quieting our domestick discords." Were he the chief "Greviance," the proclamation continued, then he announced "I will most gladly joine with them in a Petition to his Sacred Majestie to appoint a new Governor."[10] The second document was a "Declaration and Remonstrance" to justify his outlawing of Bacon who, in taking command of the frontiersmen, Berkeley maintained, had acted "against al lawes of al nations modern and ancient."[11]

Bacon, in the meantime, searched for Indians. When he and his men broke camp at Henrico, they tracked southwest until they came to the site of present-day Clarkesville, Va. There they met a tribe of friendly natives, the Occaneechees, who informed them of a nearby Susquehannock raiding party. Bacon encouraged these new found allies to attack the Susquehannocks, which they did, but then they disputed the colonists over the division of the spoils. A hot fight ensued as Bacon's men turned on the Occanneechees. As their commander later told the story, "wee regarded not the advantage of the Prisoners nor any plunder, but burn't and destroid all."[12] Bacon had at last done what Berkeley would not, or could no longer bring himself to do — slaughter Indians. His "victory" over the Occaneechees instantly turned him into the most popular man in Virginia. The timing was also perfect; it catapulted him to a seat in the House of Burgesses.

Now Bacon had to wonder if he could take his seat when the legislature convened on June 5. He was still an outlaw and subject to arrest. He prevailed on his friend Crews, who had also just been elected to the House, to go down to Jamestown to find out the governor's intentions, but Berkeley refused to meet him. However, Crews passed along the information that if Bacon came to town, some of the Council would arrange a reconciliation between the two antagonists. A wary Bacon decided against showing up alone. Taking fifty well-armed men, he sailed his sloop down the James from Curles Neck, and anchored in Sandy Bay on June 6 in range of the fort's guns. He put a man ashore with a message to Berkeley asking if he could attend the Assembly. Berkeley's answer was an order to the town gunners to sink the sloop. Their volleys drove her out of range upriver as fast as her crew could pull her off her anchorage. When darkness fell, Bacon again anchored offshore and sneaked into town to meet William Drummond and Richard Lawrence, presumably to discuss his future. The meeting lasted the night through, and dawn was breaking as Bacon hurried to regain his sloop before anyone found him out. Bad luck; someone, who saw him as he neared his longboat, gave the alarm, and the chase was on. Once aboard the sloop, the sailors tried to make good his escape, but the vessel could not elude an armed merchantman, the *Adam & Eve*. The captain, Thomas Gardiner, arrested Bacon and handed him over to the Sheriff of James City County, Theophilus Hone. In turn, Major Hone clapped his prisoner in the town jail to await Sir William's pleasure.

Days passed, and Jamestown buzzed with excitement. Knots of burgesses and townsmen whispered expectantly in the streets or over their pints. What would happen now? What would old Berkeley do? Would he imprison Bacon, or worse? And, what of Bacon's men — Would they try to break him out of jail? The answer came on June 9. That morning Berkeley convened the Council, and when it had come to order, he sent for Bacon. As Bacon entered the chamber, the governor exclaimed, "Now I behold the greatest Rebell that ever was in Virginia," to which there was no reply. Then Berkeley asked, "Sir, doe you continue to be a Gentleman, and may I take your word? if so you are at Liberty upon your owne parrol."[13] In a low voice, Bacon confessed his error. He fell to his knees, begging the governor "to grant me his Gracious Pardon," and he promised in writing to be on his "Good and Quiett behavior for one whole yeare from this date."[14] Berkeley not only pardoned his penitent cousin but he returned him to the Council, while promising him a commission within a fortnight of the legislative session's end. Days later, when Bacon pleaded his wife's illness, Berkeley even permitted him to return to Curles Neck. A crisis averted, the Assembly got back to its business.

The Assembly passed twenty statutes during its three-week session, acts that have come to be called Bacon's Laws, even though Bacon had little to do with their enactment. One supplanted the passive defense measures of March with an aggressive, more costly, scheme for combating the Indians. Another pair regulated the Indian trade and the deserted Indian lands. One was obviously aimed at colonists like those who had first prevailed on Bacon to lead them. It forbade all "unlawfull assemblies, routs riots and tumults" where "ill disposed and disaffected people" gathered "in a most apparent rebellious manner." A fourth was an act of pardon and oblivion, the design of which was to forgive all "treasons . . . done since the first day of March last past."[15] The rest of Bacon's Laws addressed local matters that had little to do with the Indian crisis. Briefly put, the legislators hoped to calm angry planters by remedying the complaints that Berkeley had invited when he called for new elections.

The meeting was nearing its end by June 23, the day Bacon and 500 men trooped into town. Quickly, some of the militia took positions at strategic points about the capital, while the main body marched to the statehouse and surrounded it. A messenger came from Berkeley to ask what Bacon wanted. Bacon requested the governor's permission to fight the Indians, thirty blank commissions for subordinate officers, a letter justifying him to Charles II, an act of pardon, a law to displace certain persons from office, and restitution for his sloop. Nothing here suggested that Bacon planned to overthrow the government.

It apeared otherwise to Berkeley. No Virginian had ever made such an ultimatum to him before, and he was in no mood to tolerate one now.

An angry Berkeley tore open his shirt and bellowed, "Shoot me!"

Bacon's demands demeaned his authority as the king's vice-regent; to accede to them invited rebellion. An angry Berkeley would yield to none of them. Enraged, he stormed out of the state house and ran up to Bacon's men. "Here," he bellowed, tearing open his shirt, "Shoot me, foregod, fair Mark, Shoot." The soldiers held steady. He then wheeled on Bacon, whom he called "a Rebell and a Traytor." Drawing his rapier, he challenged, "lett us try and end the difference singly between ourselves." "Putt it up," came the retort, as Bacon vowed that he had no desire "to hurt a haire of your honor's head." But he insisted, "God damne my Blood, I came for a commission, and a commission I shall have before I goe," and turning toward his men, gave the order, "Make ready and Present." The troops wheeled smartly, cocked their muskets, and aimed them at the statehouse. Petrified, the burgesses caved into Bacon, while some of the Council argued with Berkeley to submit as well. There was no other choice, and at length, the old man acquiesced to their importunities.[16]

Bacon's demands were perfected into law within a matter of days, and as the Assembly was winding up its business, some of the burgesses "desiered that for the satisfaction of the people, what they had don might be publickly read." Bacon curtly turned them aside, saying "there should be noe Laws read there, that he Would not admit of any delays, that he came for a Commission, and would immediately have itt." The job done,

94

Berkeley dissolved the Assembly, and Bacon, now General Bacon, got his commission.[17]

Until June 23, the governor and the general had merely disagreed over the best way to combat the Indian menace. In capturing Jamestown and extorting his commission, Bacon turned the disagreement into a struggle for control of Virginia. Berkeley was as determined to regain his power as Bacon was resolved to thwart him. The result was civil war.

Bacon marched out of Jamestown on June 26, amid fresh rumors of renewed Indian attacks on the frontier. Acting on the reports, the general sent scouting parties to locate the Indians and then rendezvous with him at the Falls of the James. Bacon and his main force made for the falls, but as they did, he received word that Berkeley had once more proclaimed him a rebel. Immediately, he turned eastward toward the capital, intent upon crushing the governor.

It was a disillusioned Berkeley who had ridden off from Jamestown some days after Bacon. He arrived at Green Spring a spent man, who for a while was content to let Bacon handle the Indians. Rest and a petition from planters in Gloucester soon brought him out of his languor. The Gloucester petitioners questioned Bacon's pressing men and supplies, which they averred left them without defenses, and they asked the governor for help. Aroused, Berkeley voided Bacon's commission, declaring it had been extracted from him as by a thief who stole his purse and made him say that he gave it up willingly. He rode over to Gloucester, where he attempted to raise some men. No one flocked to his standard because the Gloucestermen, as well as the nearby Middlesex planters, were afraid he would lead them against Bacon. Taking a few loyalists, Berkeley crossed the bay to the safety of the Eastern Shore, stunned by the realization that he could no longer command the planters' loyalties.

Bacon was back at Middle Plantation by July 29, and for the next several weeks he tried to consolidate his political hold on Virginia. He published a "Declaration of the People" and a "Manifesto," the one a harsh condemnation of Berkeley and the other a stirring justification of his own actions. Words without deeds, he knew, convinced no one. He must defeat the governor, and so, Bacon sent Giles Bland and William Carver to assault Berkeley in his stronghold at Accomack. Next, he rounded up large numbers of planters and wheedled them into obeying him and defying Berkeley until he could plead his case with King Charles II.

Satisfied that he now controlled things, Bacon again went off in search of Indians. This time the line of march took him toward the Falls of the James, but when the column picked up the trail of a tributary nation, the Pamunkeys, he changed directions and headed for the freshes of the

York. Suspected of participation in recent raids, the Pamunkeys had earlier abandoned their villages and had found refuge in the watery lowlands between Gloucester and Middlesex Counties that the English called Dragon Swamp. Locating them proved no easy matter, and as the weeks of searching through the swamp passed, the men wearied to the point where Bacon sent home those who verged on mutiny. A short while later, the militia discovered the terrified Pamunkeys and fell on them. Those who could, retreated into the depths of the swamp. An unfortunate few either were shot or made prisoner.

Even as Bacon pillaged the Pamunkeys, Berkeley chose to recapture the western shore. His lieutenant, Robert Beverley, had caught Bland and Carver, and their capture returned control of the rivers to the loyalists. Berkeley loaded his men on four ships and a dozen smaller vessels; then he sailed across the Chesapeake Bay for Jamestown, determined to retake his capital. The flotilla reached its destination on September 7, and Berkeley discovered that about 800 of Bacon's men occupied the town. He offered to exchange a pardon for their surrender, and the garrison accepted. The next day, as soon as the capitulation was completed, Berkeley retook the town and dug in to await his enemy's certain attack.

When Bacon came out of Dragon Swamp, he expected a victor's welcome for his defeat of the Pamunkeys. Instead he received the jolting news that the governor had captured Bland, Carver, and Jamestown. Pressing all the men he could find in Gloucester, Bacon hurried across the York and pushed on toward Jamestown. Arriving just north of there by the evening of September 13, he camped close to the site of the old London Company glasshouse. He and some scouts stole toward the peninsula to reconnoitre Berkeley's defenses. They were, as he soon saw, impervious to a frontal assault, and he decided to besiege them. He also played a little psychological game with Berkeley's men, some of whose wives were his prisoners. He paraded the women, together with his Indian captives, across his trenches in full view of the town's defenders. By "this subtill invention" Bacon so demoralized them that when Berkeley tried to lift the siege, his attempt failed miserably, leaving a dejected governor no option but to slink off to his stronghold in Accomack. Victorious, Bacon entered the deserted capital on September 19. He consulted with "his Cabinett Councell," after which "he in a most barberous maner [converted] the wholl Towne into flames, cinders and ashes, not so much as spareing the Church, and the first that ever was in Virginia."[18]

Destroying Jamestown lost Bacon some of his support. His stock fell still lower when he recruited bondsmen whom he promised to liberate if

BURNING OF JAMESTOWN.

Bacon entered a deserted Jamestown on September 19, 1676, and converted "the wholl Towne into flames, cinders and ashes."

they joined his cause. Having no navy, he could not get at Berkeley, so long as he stayed in Accomack. The most he could do on that score was to stir up the Eastern Shore planters, but none of them fell for that gambit. Without an enemy, he could only wait upon Sir William. Bacon waited. The longer he sat in camp the more his men grew restless. Their favorite entertainment became ransacking the estates of the loyalists, which had its own deleterious effect on Bacon's cause. As for Bacon himself, he had to decide on the revolt's future course. Should he carry on with the Indian war? Should he try to capture the governor? Should he fight the expected redcoats and strike for an independent Virginia? Should he hold out until he could defend himself before the king? Whatever his thoughts, he never betrayed them because he died quite unexpectedly on October 26 of what witnesses to his death described as the "Bloody Flux" and "Lousey Disease." His stupified followers buried him in an unmarked grave.

With Bacon dead, the revolt fell apart, despite the efforts of his most dedicated supporters. They could not sustain their cause for very long; none of them had their fallen leader's stature or ability. Berkeley took to the field as soon as he learned of the rebel's death, but he and his underlings were too inept to stamp out the rebellion's last flickerings unaided. Happily for him, half a dozen armed merchantmen had recently arrived in Virginia waters, and their skippers answered his call for help. Their assistance soon had the governor back in power.

The costs of Bacon's Rebellion were considerable. For the Indians, the revolt moved them a step closer toward their doom. For the colonists, it brought the intrusion of aggressive royal power and an eventual redefinition of their political relationships with the crown and one another. For Jamestown, it foretold decline and abandonment.

Chapter 7

Decline

The worst of Bacon's Rebellion was over by early 1677, although its embers smoldered longer than the ashes of the burned-out capital. Charles II dispatched an army of 1,000 redcoats to suppress the rebels. Berkeley had already regained control before the soldiers arrived at their destination, and there was nothing for them to do. The troops remained as an irritating reminder of the crown's renewed determination to bring Virginia nearer to its conception of empire. Berkeley and the royal commission, whom Charles sent to investigate the causes of the troubles, did not get on either. At the root of their quarrel was disagreement over who bore responsibility for the rebellion and how the ex-rebels were to be treated. The commissioners censured the governor, while they counseled leniency for Bacon's followers. Berkeley and his loyal adherents accepted none of the blame, nor was there much charity in them. Being at cross purposes only made a tense situation more taut, because the Berkeleyites controlled the colony's political structure long after Sir William sailed for London in May 1677. Their resistance to the later Stuarts' imperial policies set the tone of Virginia's politics for a generation. Inevitably, Jamestown's future intertwined with the outcome of these political skirmishes.

As for that fate, the immediate problem in 1677 was what to do with the wasted metropolis. Fire damage was extensive; no building had escaped unscathed. All of the frame dwellings were consumed. Some of the brick buildings, like the church and the statehouse complex, were gutted, although the intense heat had caused the collapse of other brick structures. Shelter for the town's permanent residents was an immediate need, as were meeting rooms for the James City County court, the General Court, and the General Assembly. Moreover, there were no longer places to house anyone who came to town on public business, let alone room to jail prisoners awaiting trial before the General Court. Until Jamestown returned to some semblance of normality, conducting the business of the government and the courts was a difficult and sometimes disorderly affair, but no one could forecast how soon the capital would be restored.

At first, there was some feeling for moving the capital to another location. That idea appeared among numerous grievances that the royal commission of investigation collected in conjuction with its inquiry into the rebellion's origins. Proponents of the move were chiefly colonists who lived far from Jamestown, along the Potomac and in the Rappahannock River valley. The most pointed of these were the freeholders of Lancaster County who urged, that for the ease of the Inhabitants of this Countrey in generall, the Generall Court for the future bee kept in some parte of *Yorke* River, it being the Center of the Countrey, the benefitt pretended or intended by building at *James* towne heretofore being never in any liklyhood equall or answerable to the greate chardge there expended long before the late unhappy fireing thereof.

Voters in Rappahannock County echoed those sentiments, although they went a bit further and argued for the "erecting townes in every County in the Collony with all Convenient speed."[1]

The commissioners dismissed the idea of moving the capital. Francis Moryson, saw promise in the suggestion for more "townes." He later lobbied royal officials for its encouragement. On their part, the members of the General Assembly of February 1677 were not impressed by the proposals either. Their chief concern, at that moment, lay in avenging themselves at the expense of the rebels. Taking the seat of government away from Jamestown had no appeal for its inhabitants either. The tavernkeepers among them depended on the custom of the politicians for much of their livelihood, just as those who served as minor functionaries in the county court, the Assembly, or the General Court did not relish the prospect of losing their jobs. The possibility of removal was stillborn, at least for the time being.

Despite the obvious necessity for Jamestown's rapid rebuilding, the colonists did not respond to the need with alacrity. Individual householders repaired or reconstructed their dwellings, as the case required, and within five or six years they had completed most of the work. The port facilities were renovated, and a few prominent colonists built new townhouses or refurbished their former ones. In April 1682, saying it was their "desyr that all Nusances and corruptions of the Air be here after removed; and the Citty for the future be kept clean and decent," Jamestown's voters petitioned the Assembly for authority to fix "certain limits and bounds" for the "metropolis of his Majesties Countrey" and to put up a storehouse.[2]

The petition's primary purpose was a further inducement to attract more of the colony's leading citizens back to town, but nothing came of the effort because the Assembly never acted on the request. Even had the petition passed into law, the value of its effect would have been doubtful. As Governor Thomas, Lord Culpeper observed, all earlier attempts were "in vaine," because the big men saw no advantage in living in town, and nothing the petitioners proposed sweetened the attraction. Failure to lure prominent Virginians back to Jamestown was in accord with the slow revitalization of the fort, the church, the governor's residence, the capitol complex, and the other public facilities.

When repairs to the fort began is uncertain, although they were obviously completed before the Rev. John Clayton described its condition in a letter he wrote to the Royal Society in 1688. Clayton, who took up the rectorship at the Jamestown church six years earlier, commented,

> Now they have built a silly sort of a Fort, that is, a Brick wall in the shape of a Half-Moon, at the beginning of the Swamp [i.e., Pitch and Tar], because the Channel of the River lies very nigh the Shoar; but it is the same as if a Fort were built at *Chelsea* to secure London from being taken by shipping. Besides Ships passing up the River are secured from the Guns of the Fort, till they come directly over-against the Fort, by reason the Fort stands in a Vale, and all the Guns directed down the River, that should play on the Ships, as they are coming up the River will lodge their Shot within ten, twenty, or forty Yards in the rising Bank, which is much above the Level of the Fort; so that if a Ship gave but a good Broad-side just when she comes to bear upon the Fort, she might put the Fort into that Confusion, as to have free Passage enough.[3]

Parishioners put the church right by 1680. The governor's residence was never rebuilt. Until restoration on the capitol complex commenced in 1684, neither the General Assembly, the General Court, nor the James City County court had regular meeting places. All three bodies returned to Jamestown in 1680, when there were enough refurbished private buildings to house them. Usually, officials contracted with the town's publicans for space in their taverns. Ann Macon, for example, provided the "Assembly Room [and] the two Chambers over head for the Clerkes office and the Committee Chambers" whenever the legislature sat, while Henry Gawler or William Armiger furnished rooms for Council sessions.[4]

These arrangements sufficed until the opening of a partially rebuilt statehouse in 1685. Construction began on the new structure shortly after Governor Francis, Lord Howard of Effingham took up his government in the spring of 1684. That May, the House of Burgesses approved a committee recommendation authorizing William Sherwood "to draw the Articles between his Excellency and the Speaker in behalfe of the Generall Assembly And the Honorable Col. *phillip Ludwell* for the Rebuilding the state house."[5] Within a year and a half, the work had proceeded to a point where housing was available for the Council and the Assembly, their clerks, and the Secretary of the Colony, but more than another decade passed before Ludwell completed the unfinished building.

Such seeming sloth requires explanation. It certainly did not result from indolence or want of craftsmen and construction materials. Virginia was home to numerous men skilled in the builders' trades. Governor Berkeley, who had employed armies of house builders developing his beloved Green Spring, knew as much when he told Francis Moryson in the spring of 1677 how quickly the repairs to Jamestown might be accomplished. "If there are Carpenters and Oxen or Horses to draw in the Timber," he said, "ten houses, att least, may be built in a day."[6] Furthermore, brick and lime kilns flourished on the island before the fire. Given their design, whatever fire damage those kilns sustained would not have been difficult to repair. Abundant quantities of lumber were also readily available; if not on the island itself, then within easy reach of the building sites.

If not laziness and shortages of laborers or want of supplies, then what caused the delays? In a word, politics. After 1677, any plans to restore the government buildings were held hostage by colonial politicians who resisted the crown's attempts to force them into accepting Stuart conceptions of empire.

For one thing, the members of the post-rebellion General Assemblies were reluctant to increase taxes to pay for the costs of restoration. Their reluctance was understandable. Back in the 1660s, the Assembly had raised enormous sums to encourage Jamestown's development, but their outlay achieved modest results while adding hugely to the ordinary planters' already heavy tax burden. Those levies were, after all, one of the grievances that led to the upheaval of 1676, and that was an experience the burgesses were not quick to forget. Virginia's economy stagnated into the 1680s. Straitened economic conditions kept green the memories of Bacon's Rebellion, just as they made any tax hike difficult.

Then too, the leaders turned to the freeholders for help in checking Stuart interference in Virginia's political arrangements. Such support required coming to terms with the small planters, and one of these was greater solicitude for their constituents' interests. Once they struck their bargain with the voters, the great men had greater leeway to stymie the most visible symbol of the crown's intrusive authority — the royal governor.

Post-rebellion governors were of a different breed than Sir William Berkeley. Berkeley had his way because he carefully cultivated those Virginians who dominated colonial politics and presumed to speak for all. He became one of them, while, for the most part, he ignored his masters in England. In his prime, he knew Virginia's political terrain as few colonial governors did. His successors lacked both his knowledge and his willingness to join their interests with Virginia's ruling groups. Their loyalties were to Charles II, James II, and William and Mary, whose visions of empire they shared and to whom they looked for preferment. Openly contemptuous of men they took to be ignorant, Sir

Herbert Jeffreys, Culpeper, Effingham, Francis Nicholson, and Sir Edmund Andros displayed little inclination to appreciate the subtle shadings of late seventeenth-century Virginia politics. Instead, they were determined to bend the Virginians to their sovereign's wishes. Thus, they presided over a colony in which the politics of confrontation was the frequent order of the day.

Two issues — rebuilding a governor's mansion and a renewed interest in promoting the development of towns — illustrate the intimacy of the relationship between the reconstruction of Jamestown and politics. Because Jeffreys's tenure was short, Culpeper was the first of the post-rebellion governors to confront these issues. His lordship showed little concern for having a mansion, but then he spent more of his administration in England than in the colony. On those occasions when he stayed any length of time, he took up residence at Green Spring where he and the widowed Lady Frances Berkeley, as he put it, "live frankly together without any of your European selvishness, or politick coveteousness, to disturb us."[7] In short, he never pressed the Assembly to vote funds for the house. It was different with Effingham.

A man of modest means, Effingham viewed the mansion as one of the tempting perquisites of office. Moreover, he saw it as a visible, necessary symbol of the vigorous royal authority that he represented. A great house, built and maintained by colonial taxes, would remind obstreperous colonists of their duty and dependence on the king, their master. He tried unsuccessfully to wheedle an appropriation from his first General Assembly; he settled instead for what was supposed to be an interim housing allowance. As relations between Effingham and leading Virginians soured to where they were irretrievably poisoned, the matter of the governor's house got lost in the squabbles. Effingham's successors seem not to have broached the matter. Instead, they were content to stay with which ever Virginian would lodge them.

Charles II sent Culpeper to Virginia with instructions to secure the passage of legislation that would encourage the growth of towns throughout Virginia. Without towns, Culpeper remarked in his opening speech to the General Assembly of 1680, "noe other nation [has] ever begunne a plantation or any yet thrived (as it ought)."[8] Artfully, the governor surmounted his opposition and secured adoption of a bill that authorized the creation of twenty towns, each to be situated on the colony's water highways. Of course, Jamestown was to be one of these. The crown disallowed the statute; thus when Effingham succeeded Culpeper, he brought with him an instruction for new town legislation. He failed to get it carried into law during the General Assembly of 1684, but he was determined to enact it when he called the Assembly to meet in late 1685. That was not to be. The burgesses arrived at Jamestown in an angry

The Fourth State House did not escape the fire that consumed Jamestown on October 31, 1698.

mood over earlier disagreements with Effingham, and soon they quarreled with him over the wording of the new town bill. Their disputes turned the meeting into the rowdiest Assembly of any in the seventeenth century, which ultimately forced Effingham to prorogue it without any legislation becoming law. Six years passed before another governor attempted to broach the subject of towns anew.

Slowed by political bickering, Jamestown's recovery inched along. The Rev. James Blair reported to the Board of Trade in 1697 how the capital then boasted of about thirty houses, a renovated church, a stout jail, and a nearly completed statehouse. Outwardly, things appeared as though they had at last returned to their condition before Nathaniel Bacon set the town afire. A closer look revealed otherwise. No longer was Jamestown Virginia's sole port or even its only town. Since 1680, other port towns — Urbanna, Norfolk, Yorktown, and Hobbes Hole (now Tappahannock) — had sprung up. Their existence did not foreshadow the urbanization of the Old Dominion, but the swift growth in the number of their inhabitants and the volume of commerce signaled the decline of the ancient metropolis's pre-eminence.

The end came sooner than any of its inhabitants should have expected. Fire struck on October 31, 1698, and within hours, Jamestown again lay mostly in ashes. The next year Governor Nicholson persuaded the General Assembly to move the seat of government inland to a site at Middle Plantation that grew into the city of Williamsburg.

104

Chapter 8

Since 1699

Now the capital was gone, and with it went Jamestown's reason for being. Slowly, the metropolis slipped into decay before it disappeared altogether. About twenty householders, — the town's permanent residents — stayed on. So did their descendants, but their number dwindled. Hugh Jones, an English parson who served as rector at Jamestown, wrote in *The Present State of Virginia*, published in 1724, that Jamestown consisted "at present of nothing but an abundance of brick rubbish, and three or four good inhabited houses."[1] (Nearby residents carted off the "rubbish" and used it for their own homes or other purposes.) Jamestown's inhabitants moved away or died before the end of the Revolution, and when the last of them left, the town was no more.

After 1699, the few qualified voters among the villagers continued to send a burgess to Williamsburg. Their right to their own representative in the House of Burgesses was a concession to their town's former pre-eminence, but even this last dignity disappeared in 1776. By then, Jamestown had become the nearest thing to a rotten borough as there was in colonial Virginia, and in their ardor for republican principles, Virginia's revolutionaries stripped away this vestige of seeming political corruption when they drafted a constitution for the independent commonwealth.

Faithful parishioners maintained the church for some fifty years into the eighteenth century, actually, their number even rose during the century's early decades. After coming to Jamestown, the Rev. Mr. Jones remarked on his parish as being "of pretty large extent," though he noted that its size was "less than others."[2] His latter observation proved prophetic because even as he wrote it, the Church of England was losing ground to newer sects that sprang up all across Virginia before the Revolution. Jones soon left the Jamestown church for a cure in Maryland, and after he departed, its membership fell dramatically. Despite the decline, the parish struggled along until 1758, when it was finally abandoned. The building remained vacant for another half-century before John Ambler, who received some money from a bequest left by William Ludwell Lee of Green Spring, pulled it down and used some of its bricks to construct the wall that presently surrounds the graveyard. From that day to this, the church tower has stood as Jamestown's sole surviving seventeenth-century structure.[3]

Although the town's end came legally and physically during the Revolution, the island was not completely abandoned at that time. Well before the capital's removal to Williamsburg, land on the island was being consolidated into the hands of a few families who eventually converted the whole of it to agricultural uses. Of these, the Travis family

105

The first brick church built in Jamestown, 1639. The tower was added after 1647.

had the longest roots. The first of their holdings antedated 1650. Thereafter, succeeding generations of Travises acquired more until their acreage comprised a sizeable tract downriver in the area bounded by the Back River and Passmore Creek. No trace of the Travises' house exists. Even its location remains in doubt, though it may be near the family burial ground, which is still visible. The family appears to have abandoned the dwelling after a fire destroyed it either in 1822 or 1857, depending on which tradition one chooses to believe.

William Sherwood and Edward Jaquelin were among the other early major landowners. A late seventeenth-century politician of some prominence, Sherwood amassed his holdings between the 1676 fire and his death in 1697. Sherwood's properties subsequently passed to Jaquelin, who added them to his own. In turn, the combined Sherwood-Jaquelin tract came to Richard Ambler through his marriage to one of the Jaquelins. His family lived in a large plantation house, whose remnant is now Jamestown's most conspicuous ruin. Erected before 1720, the mansion was planned in a style that Tidewater planters began to favor before that date: a dominant central structure flanked by dependencies to give the whole edifice line, proportion, and balance. That design, which today is recognized as characteristic of the Georgian architectural style, became a distinctive characteristic of Virginia's eighteenth-century

The church tower stands as Jamestown's sole surviving 17th Century structure. Inside the Memorial Church are the brick and cobblestone foundations of the 1617 frame church and the brick foundation of the 1639 church.

stately homes, and it bespoke their owners' belief in a rationally ordered universe. By the time the last in a series of fires forced the Ambler House's abandonment in 1895, the whole of the island had been under single ownership for more than sixty years, and it was farmed continuously until the 1920s.

Armed conflict, which had caused so much destruction in 1676, briefly returned to Jamestown during both the War for Independence and the Civil War. Following the Battle of Guilford Courthouse in March 1781, Charles, Lord Cornwallis abandoned North Carolina for Virginia, thereby setting a course that ultimately led him to his rendezvous with destiny at Yorktown. By July, Cornwallis's army lay on the Peninsula just above Jamestown, and its rear guard seemed a tempting target to the Americans. Their commander, the young, impetuous Marquis de Lafayette, ordered an assault on July 6, which the British easily repulsed, but the skirmish hastened Cornwallis toward his fate. Two months later, just as George Washington was about to spring his trap on Cornwallis, elements of Jean, Comte de Rochambeau's army landed on the island, where they camped for a night before marching across the Peninsula to

The Jacquelin-Ambler ruins as photographed in May 1938. The roomy brick structure was built about 1710.

In 1861, during the American Civil War, Confederate soldiers threw up earthworks on Jamestown Island to defend against a likely Union assault on Richmond.

link up with the main body of the attacking force that besieged the British.

Eighty years later, Confederate soldiers threw up earthworks on the island to defend against a likely Union assault on Richmond via the James. Rebel engineers placed one of the forts, a rectangular redoubt, in the vicinity of the former Travis properties at the head of Passmore Creek. (Except for an overgrowth of trees and wearing from exposure to the elements, it is intact.) To the west, they dug another bastion, locating it near the spot that tradition held as the site of the first settlers' fort. (Its remaining parts lie immediately beyond the church.) A road, traces of which may be seen even now, linked the two. The engineers also constructed rifle pits on the high ground along the island's northwest edge to discourage attackers who might wish to approach from the mainland. (You can still see some of them.) These fortifications never fulfilled their intended purpose; none figured in any of the war's major campaigns. And yet, for twentieth-century Americans, there is symbolism in their remains. They serve as mute souvenirs from a horrible conflict that ended an inhuman labor system that the colonists began at Jamestown.

Well before the Civil War, Jamestown had already assumed a symbolic coloration of a different sort. Antebellum Americans considered it a romantic emblem of their nationhood. Accordingly, whereas the colonists took no notice of the centenary of Jamestown's founding, their nineteenth-century descendants regularly observed the anniversaries of the first landing. These celebrations were generally low-key affairs, consisting of little more than some clergy, public men, and a few spectators gathering on the island for prayers and speeches. Marking the bicentennial and the two hundred-fiftieth anniversaries called for a more elaborate kind of commemoration. The Jubilee of 1807 set a pattern for all of its successors.

Virginians from Norfolk, Petersburg, Portsmouth, and Norfolk formed a committee to organize the jubilee. They arranged a five-day affair with activities divided among Jamestown, Williamsburg, and private homes. Festivities included the obligatory ceremony at the site of the abandoned capital, plus a parade, a bazaar, and a regatta, all of which were interspersed with speeches and odes delivered by local politicians or students from the College of William and Mary. Speakers remarked on the relationship between Jamestown and liberty, the early colonists' desperate struggle, and the promise of the country's future. Their words struck the receptive ears of listeners who reveled in a style of oratory that to us seems overblown, but such public discourse was one of the few forms of popular entertainment in that day. The organizers knew that food and partying drew crowds too — the observance's culminating events were a picnic and a series of dances held at nearby plantations. Considering how difficult it was to travel at the time, the number of people who participated in the bicentennial — several hundred according to the committee's own report — was remarkable.

Travel was much easier by 1857, which made Jamestown more accessible to those who wished to partake of the two hundred-fiftieth anniversary observances. More than eight thousand people attended a celebration that numbered among its participants ex-President John Tyler, a Charles City County native, and Henry A. Wise, the Commonwealth's incumbent governor. Tyler reminisced about how, as an undergraduate at the College of William and Mary, he had sometimes wandered among the village's moldering ruins while he reflected on past glories and future promises. In his address, Wise, a man whose own lifetime coincided with the expansion of the nation's boundaries to California, reminded his audience how they could "go to the Pacific now to measure the progression and power of a great people."[4]

There were also sixteen companies of militia from across the Old Dominion who paraded to the delight of the crowd. Such drills always added color, frivolity, romance, and excitement to any public occasion, and this was no exception. Only a prophet could have foreseen in the militiamen's exercise a rehearsal for civil war, but the audience numbered no soothsayers that day.

Planning for Jamestown's tercentenary commenced with the opening of the twentieth century. Encouraged by state officials, the planners envisioned a celebration resembling those of the past, but things did not work out as expected. Others, who wished to promote the lower James River basin for its industrial and commercial possibilities, dreamed of an exposition akin to those mounted in Atlanta and New Orleans in the 1880s. Their view prevailed. The Jamestown Exposition of 1907, replete with temporary exhibition halls filled to capacity with a myriad of products, was held on the site of the modern Norfolk Naval Base rather than at "the cradle of the republic." Excursion steamers regularly ran venturesome tourists upriver to witness exercises such as the dedications of the Tercentenary Monument and the Memorial Church. Afflicted with crippling financial difficulties, the exposition proved less promising than its promoters had imagined.

The most recent of these major celebrations occurred in 1957, and was engineered through the combined efforts of the state and federal governments. This time, planners heeded the counsel of a surviving director of the 1907 festival who suggested that "we do not have a stereotyped, old-style commercial exposition." They opted instead for a commemoration of "dignified and historic" proportions.[5] Their scheme succeeded, and the Jamestown Festival of 1957, which ran for eight months, drew an estimated attendance of 2.1 million visitors, among whom were Queen Elizabeth II, her husband, Prince Philip, and assorted dignitaries from around the globe.

As important as the festival itself were its many residual benefits. Among the more remarkable of these was the work of a group of early American historians who proposed and carried out a project to microfilm Virginia's colonial records in foreign depositories. Another was the preparation of a series of historical studies about seventeenth-century Virginia. Archaeologists conducted extensive on-site excavations. Construction of the Colonial Parkway from Williamsburg to Jamestown was finished, a causeway rejoined the island to the mainland, and a new visitor center was built. These improvements represented the culmination of years of effort to stay the island's erosion into the James and to transform the vestiges of the ancient town into a shrine that befitted its historic stature.

The shoreline had held its shape over the seventeenth century,

Then Vice President Richard Nixon (second from right) was one of the dignitaries to attend the 350th Anniversary Festival.

111

although wind-driven tides sometimes flooded across the isthmus and temporarily cut off the "greate road." However, erosion of land accelerated after the century turned, and by the time the French military engineer, Col. Desandrouins, mapped the island's northwestern end in 1781, the isthmus was no more. Wakes from nineteenth-century steamboats contributed to a problem that no one quite knew how to stop, or cared to, at least until the formation of the Association for the Preservation of Virginia Antiquities in 1889. A women's organization dedicated to the protection of the "ancient historic grounds, buildings, monuments, and tombs in the Commonwealth of Virginia," the APVA hoped to save Jamestown's remains by stabilizing the ruins and the shoreline. That aspiration came closer to reality in 1893, when the landowners gave the association a parcel of 22.5 acres that encompassed the church tower and the western end of the old town site. Shortly thereafter, the United States Corps of Engineers retained Colonel Samuel H. Yonge to construct a concrete seawall. Yonge completed the wall in 1906, but another three decades passed before the Civilian Conservation Corps built the riprap retaining wall that runs from the eastern end of Yonge's construction to a point below Orchard Run. In the intervening years, storms, excessive tides, and heavy rains washed still more land away. According to most estimates, more than 700 feet of shoreline was lost to erosion between 1607 and 1935.

The APVA had sole responsibility for conserving Jamestown as a historic site until the 1930s. By soliciting contributions from private individuals and patriotic organizations, it was able to raise funds for landscaping, restoration, and even some limited reconstruction. Its most visible achievements came as part of the 1907 exposition. The association donated the land for the Tercentenary Monument, and persuaded the National Society of the Colonial Dames of America to erect the Memorial Church on the foundations of the 1639 building. Clearly, without the dedication of the committed women of the APVA, Jamestown might well have completely fallen into the river.

In 1934, the United States Department of the Interior acquired the balance of the island and placed its management under the control of the National Park Service as part of the Colonial National Monument. An act of Congress in 1936 changed the designation to that of a national historical park. Four years later, the Park Service and the APVA agreed to a unified program of administration and development. The arrangement governs the management of Jamestown to this day.

A side benefit of the Corps of Engineers' employment of Colonel Yonge was his interest in archaeology. Archaeology was still in its infancy in Yonge's time, and its practitioners were more preoccupied with discovering classical or pre-Columbian antiquities than they were

112

engaged by the prospect of finding the artifacts of America's European settlers. Following in the footsteps of Mary Anne Galt, Mary Winder Garrett, and John Tyler, Jr., Yonge conducted the first extensive fieldwork to see what evidence of Jamestown's past lay buried beneath the ground. He located the foundations of the Ludwell statehouse group, which he described in his book, *The Site of Old "James Towne," 1607-1698.* His techniques were primitive — he seems not to have considered the evidentiary value of potsherds or the other bits and pieces of the colonists' material possessions. He made no precise notation of the things he unearthed, nor of their exact location, although he linked his digging to research in the documentary records available to him. In that respect, he anticipated an important element in what is know called "historical archeology;" that is, the marriage between written records and artifacts. His digs also pointed to the probability of more discoveries and the likelihood that excavating the townsite could yield answers for hitherto unresolved questions about the town, the lives of its inhabitants, and their material culture.

Yonge never pursued these possibilities. The APVA had no money to sustain an extended dig. Consequently, these early archaeological explorations ended once the colonel concluded his work, and further discoveries lay buried until 1934.

In that year, Park Service archaeologists undertook the first of two major excavations of "James Cittie." Their approach to the problem, compared to Yonge's, was quite sophisticated. Their techniques may be said to be among the pioneering work of modern historical archaeology. They assembled teams of engineers, architects, conservation technicians, historians, and laborers to survey the island and to make preparations for the dig. The unearthing proceeded in an ordered, systematic fashion. As of 1938, there were storage facilities and a field laboratory where specialists could process and analyze the items that the earth yielded. Diminishing funds and the onset of World War II caused the work to dwindle until the middle 1950s, when it picked up anew.

A principal object of the second phase of the excavations was the pinpointing of the first fort, which the Confederates had presumably covered in 1861. The search failed to produce unimpeachable results, though three bits of evidence appear to have confirmed the traditional location as the likeliest spot. One was the discovery of debris, within the perimeters of the rebel fort, from an armorer's forge that dated to 1620, if not earlier. Another was the finding of nearby burial grounds whose occupants were hastily interred before the end of the seventeenth-century's second decade. These things hinted that the fort may have been in the immediate vicinity, but on ground that had washed away. Would soldiers, the reasoning went, stray far from the safety of the fort to repair

In 1934, the National Park Service undertook the first of two major excavations of "James Cittie." The teams of engineers, architects, conservation technicians, historians, and laborers

surveyed the island and the unearthing proceeded in an ordered, systematic fashion. At the storage facilities and a field laboratory specialists processed and analyzed the items that the earth yielded.

Dr. John L. Cotter, NPS Chief Archeologist, with the "pile driver" discovered during the second phase of the excavations in the mid-1950s.

their weapons or bury their dead? Finally, there were the negative results from the investigation of an alternative site, the Elay-Swann tract, which was located on the shore of the James about half a mile southeast of the church. Scholars theorized in the 1930s that the first fort may have stood on a triangular stretch of ground at this spot, but test trenches done in 1937 failed to substantiate their speculation, and it was not verified by more extensive exploration of the area in 1955.

Additional investigations were conducted at the church, the statehouses, and assorted other locations, but these by no means exhausted all of the possibilities. The excavating ended in time for the Jamestown Festival. There have been no digs since then.

More than half a century of exploration has uncovered literally tons of artifacts. Some of these are displayed at the Visitor Center. Individually and collectively, the objects help to cut a clearer image of life in the little colonial capital. The digs themselves provided a picture of how the town was laid out, and how it changed. They also reveal where its principal buildings sat and what their probable uses might have been. In that way, the archaeological fieldwork deepened our understanding of an era so removed by time and outlook from our own.

Although reconstructing Jamestown was considered in the past, that idea has long since been abandoned in favor of presenting the townsite and the island's wilderness as the real exhibit. Today, the spot on which the metropolis once stood is a serenely quiet place. Its antiquity and significance tug at the imagination. Standing in the churchyard, or pausing beside an exposed foundation, the mindful visitor can almost imagine himself amidst the bustle of "James Cittie in Virginia" in its heyday.

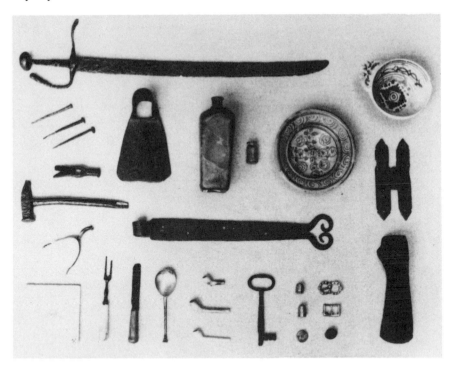

More than half a century of explorations has uncovered literally tons of artifacts. These objects help to cut a clearer image of life in the little colonial capital.

117

Epilogue

Why did the metropolis on the James founder when Boston, New York, Philadelphia, and Charleston all succeeded? Like them, it sat amidst an abundant land. Like them, it sheltered determined colonists. Like them, it was unsanitary and disease ridden. Nothing about these shared characteristics explains the failure. Instead, the answer lies in the ways in which Jamestown differed from the others. Geography conspired against it. Bad luck damned it. Fire consumed it. It waxed and waned, and it was no more.

Jamestown Memorial Cross

119

A Jamestown Chronology

1497–1498
John Cabot and his three sons explored the North American coast and established an English claim to the continent.

1501–1504
Anglo-Portuguese voyages made from Bristol to Newfoundland.

1509–1570s
North America visited sporadically by English fishermen, but the English had little interest in building on their findings or earlier New World discoveries.

1577–1580
Sir Francis Drake circumnavigated the earth.

1576–1578
Martin Frobisher tried to find the Northwest Passage.

1578–1583
Sir Humphrey Gilbert attempted to colonize Newfoundland.

1584
Sir Walter Ralegh sent Philip Amadas and Arthur Barlowe to locate a suitable site for a colony. They landed at Roanoke Island, N.C., and Ralegh named the area "Virginia" in honor of Queen Elizabeth I.

1585
Ralegh dispatched another group of colonists to Roanoke Island.

1587
Ralegh sent the "Lost Colony" to Roanoke Island.

1588–1604
The Anglo-Spanish War prevented relief of the Roanoke Island colonists and helped end Ralegh's interest in colonization.

1606
King James I granted the London Company a charter to found a colony in the New World. The Jamestown voyage began in December when three vessels laden with supplies and 105 colonists set sail for America.

1607
The London Company ships raised the Chesapeake Bay in April. After several weeks of exploring, the colonists landed at Jamestown Island on May 13 and began constructing a settlement. Capt. Christopher Newport returned to England for a first supply of stores

and colonists. The Indians captured John Smith and held him prisoner for several months.

1608

Newport returned with the first supply. Fire nearly consumed Jamestown. John Smith became President of the Council. The first women, a Mrs. Forest and Ann Burras, arrived as colonists.

1609

John Smith was wounded and forced to return to England for treatment. The London Company was reorganized and granted a new charter.

1609-1610

The winter of "the starving time."

1610

Sir Thomas Gates landed and decided to abandon Jamestown, but the arrival of Governor Thomas West, Lord De la Warr saved the colony.

1611

"Sick upon the point to leave the world," Governor De La Warr departed Jamestown on March 28. Sir Thomas Dale relieved Deputy-Governor George Percy later that spring and began the rigorous enforcement of the modified code of military discipline known as *The Lawes Divine, Morall and Martiall.*

1611–1613

John Rolfe conducted his experiments with growing West Indian tobacco.

1612

The London Company received its third charter on March 12.

1613

Samuel Argall captured Powhatan's daughter, Pocahontas, for a hostage in April.

1614

After Pocahontas converted to Christianity, she and John Rolfe were married on April 5 in the Jamestown church. Rolfe shipped his first cargo of tobacco to England.

1616

Pocahontas, now called Rebecca, and John Rolfe sailed to England together with Sir Thomas Dale and a company of Indians.

1617

Pocahontas died and was buried at Gravesend, England; Rolfe returned to Virginia.

1618

Powhatan died; his brother, Itopatin, succeeded him as great *werowance*. The London Company was reorganized under the leadership of its new treasurer Sir Edwin Sandys. Company officials appointed George Yeardley governor to replace the deceased Lord De la Warr, and they drew up new instructions — the so-called "Great Charter" — in an attempt to salvage the failing colony.

1619

Opechancanough replaced Itopatin as great *werowance* and began to make plans to drive the English from his homeland. Governor Yeardley started the construction of "the New Towne." In July, the first General Assembly convened in the "quire" of the Jamestown church. A month later, the skipper of a Dutch man-o'-war sold a cargo of some twenty Africans in Virginia. The London Company recruited a hundred young women for wives and sent them to Jamestown in November. Of these, ninety landed in the spring of 1620.

1621

Sir Francis Wyatt succeeded Yeardley as governor. He instituted quarterly sessions of courts, among other authorized improvements in the colony's government. Another thirty-eight "maids for wives" landed.

1622

Opechancanough and his warriors attacked the colony on Friday, March 22, killing about one-third of Virginia's English population. War between the English and the Indians dragged on for nearly a decade thereafter. The plague followed the "massacre" and by 1623 only about 300 English settlers were left in Virginia.

1624

The crown seized the London Company's charter, thereby setting the stage for Virginia becoming a royal colony. An Act of Assembly provided for the establishment of monthly courts to try petty civil causes; these were the forerunners of the county courts.

1625

James I died and was succeeded by his son, Charles I, who proclaimed Virginia a royal colony. Sir Francis Wyatt became Virginia's first royal governor.

1626

Charles I appointed Sir George Yeardley to succeed Sir Francis Wyatt.

1627

Governor Yeardley died. The Virginia Council of State elected Francis West as acting governor, thereby establishing the precedent of having the senior councilor act whenever the governor died or vacated his post.

1632

The General Assembly undertook its first revision of the colony's statute law.

1634

Virginia was divided into eight counties. Each had a court that met monthly and consisted of justices of the peace, a clerk, and a sheriff. The creation of the counties marked the beginnings of the colony's tradition of vibrant local government.

1635

The "thrusting out" of Governor Sir John Harvey by his opponents in the Council of State.

1639–1641

Construction of the fourth, or first brick, Jamestown church.

1639

Charles I legitimated the General Assembly and named Sir Francis Wyatt to replace Sir John Harvey as governor.

1641

Sir William Berkeley commissioned governor.

1642

Governor Berkeley landed in Virginia.

1643

The General Assembly completed its second revision of colonial law.

1644

Opechancanough mounted another strike at the English. His initial attack killed 500 colonists and touched off a war that lasted until 1646. Opechancanough was among the casualties; he was murdered while a prisoner in the Jamestown jail.

1649

The Puritans executed Charles I. Berkeley and the General Assembly proclaimed the colony's loyalty to the Stuart monarchy and recognized Charles II as their king.

1650

Parliament passed a law forbidding English trade with Virginia to force the colonists' acceptance of the Cromwellian regime.

1651

Parliament adopted a navigation act aimed at regulating trade between England and the colonies. This statute became the precedent for the Restoration-era trade laws.

1652

Governor Berkeley averted civil war when he surrendered Virginia to a parliamentary commission who had arrived off Jamestown in a squadron of naval vessels. Richard Bennet became governor, and the General Assembly revised the laws a third time.

1652–1660, The Interregnum

Royalist sentiment remained high as most Virginians preferred the Stuart monarchy rather than a Puritan commonwealth. During these years, the powers of the General Assembly increased. There were renewed efforts at spurring the growth of Jamestown as the colony's only town. The General Assembly revised the statutes again in 1658. When Oliver Cromwell died the Puritan regime in England unraveled.

1660

The General Assembly chose Sir William Berkeley governor in March after Samuel Mathews, the last Interregnum governor, died. Charles II was restored to his throne in May, and he recommissioned Berkeley. Parliament enacted the first of the Restoration-era navigation laws.

1661

An election for the House of Burgesses was held in March. This was the last general election until June 1676. Governor Berkeley went to England to lobby against Stuart imperial policy and to advance his own scheme for diversifying Virginia's economy.

1662

The General Assembly made its fifth revision of colonial law.

1667

In the midst of the Second Anglo-Dutch War, a squadron of Dutch warships sailed into the Chesapeake Bay and captured thirteen tobacco ships. Their attack led to the rebuilding of the Jamestown fort.

1677

Dutch men-o'-war raided in the James River during the Third Anglo-Dutch War.

1675

A party of Doeg Indians attacked English settlements in Stafford County and set off the events that led to Bacon's Rebellion.

1676

Bacon's Rebellion broke out across Virginia and plunged the colony into civil war. Jamestown was burned.

1677–1698

Post-rebellion governors tried to rebuild Jamestown, but with little success. Philip Ludwell reconstructed the statehouse.

1698

A fire destroyed the statehouse and the surrounding town.

1699

Governor Francis Nicholson and the General Assembly decided to move the capital to Middle Plantation, soon to be known as Williamsburg. Thereafter, the island reverted to private owners who converted it to farming.

1781

French troops landed at Jamestown and marched to Yorktown, where they joined Washington to defeat Lord Cornwallis's army.

1807

Citizens from Norfolk, Petersburg, Portsmouth, and Williamsburg commemorated the bicentennial anniversary of Jamestown's founding.

1857

Some six thousand persons attended ceremonies that marked Jamestown's two-hundred and fiftieth anniversary.

1861

Confederate earthworks were constructed near the presumed site of the original Jamestown fort.

1893

The Association for the Preservation of Virginia Antiquities acquired title to 22.5 acres of the western end of the island, which included the sites of the 1639 brick church and the last statehouse.

1901–1903

Mary Anne Galt, Mary Winder Garrett, John Tyler, Jr., and Col. Samuel H. Yonge conducted the first archaeological excavations at Jamestown.

1907

A Jamestown Exposition was held in Norfolk to commemorate the tercentennial anniversary of Jamestown's founding. The 1639 brick church was reconstructed on its original foundations, and the Tercentenary Monument was erected on land donated by the APVA.

1934

All of Jamestown Island, except for the APVA property, became part of the Colonial National Historical Park.

1934–1941

National Park Service archaeologists undertook the first phase of the major excavations at Jamestown.

1954–1957

The second major digs were conducted.

1957

The 350th Anniversary Festival commemorated the founding of the first permanent English settlement in America.

Appendix I
Virginia's Chief Executives, 1607–1699
Presidents of the Council

Edward Maria Wingfield, 1607
John Ratcliffe, 1607-1608
John Smith, 1608-1609
George Percy, 1609-1610

Company Governors

[*Note: A lieutenant-governor was commissioned by the Company whereas an acting or deputy-governor was named by the governor or the lieutenant to act in his stead.*]

Thomas West, 3d Lord De la Warr, 1610–1618
Lieutenant-Governor Sir Thomas Gates, 1610
Deputy-Governor George Percy, 1611
Deputy-Governor Sir Thomas Dale, 1611
Lieutenant-Governor Sir Thomas Gates, 1611–1614
Deputy-Governor Sir Thomas Dale, 1614–1616
Deputy-Governor George Yeardley,1616–1617
Acting Governor Samuel Argall, 1617–1619
Deputy-Governor Nathaniel Powell, 1619
Sir George Yeardley, 1619–1621
Sir Francis Wyatt, 1621–1625

Royal Governors

[*Note: Royal governors were customarily styled "His Majesty's Governor and Captain-General" to signify their military as well as political authority. A lieutenant-governor usually held a royal commission, whereas the deputy was named by the governor. In the governor's absence, or when there was neither a lieutenant nor a deputy-governor, the President of the Council of State — the senior member — acted as governor.*]

Sir Francis Wyatt, 1625–1626
Sir George Yeardley, 1626–1627
President Francis West, 1627–1629
President Dr. John Pott, 1629–1630
Sir John Harvey, 1630–1635
President John West, 1635–1637
Sir John Harvey, 1637–1639
Sir Francis Wyatt, 1639–1642
Sir William Berkeley, 1642–1652

Commonwealth Governors

[*Note: During the Interregnum, the House of Burgesses chose the governor.*]

Richard Bennett, 1652–1655
Edward Digges, 1655–1656
Samuel Mathews, II, 1656–1660
Sir William Berkeley, 1660

Royal Governors

Sir William Berkeley, 1660-1677
Deputy-Governor Francis Moryson, 1661–1662
Deputy-Governor Sir Henry Chicheley, 1674–1682
Sir Herbert Jeffreys, 1677–1678
Thomas Lord Culpeper, 1677–1683
President Nicholas Spencer, 1683–1684
Francis, Lord Howard of Effingham, 1683–1692
President Nathaniel Bacon, 1684–1690
Lieutenant-Governor Francis Nicholson, 1690–1692
Sir Edmund Andros, 1692–1698
President Ralph Wormeley, II, 1693
Francis Nicholson, 1698–1705

Source: W. W. Abbot, comp., *A Virginia Chronology, 1585–1783* [Jamestown 350th Anniversary Booklets, Williamsburg, Va., 1957], 74-75.

Appendix II

Speakers of the House of Burgesses, 1643–1699*

Thomas Stegge, 1643
Edward Hill, 1645–1646,
   1654–1655, 1659
Edmund Scarburgh, I,
   1645–1646
Ambrose Harmer, 1646
Thomas Harwood, 1647–1649
Edward Major, 1652
Thomas Dew, 1652
Walter Chiles, 1653
William Whitby, 1653
Francis Moryson, 1656
John Smith, 1658**
Theoderick Bland, 1660

Henry Soanes, 1661
Robert Wynne, 1662–1674
Thomas Godwin, 1676
Augustine Warner, 1676, 1677
William Travers, 1677
Mathew Kemp, 1679
Thomas Ballard, 1680–1682
Edward Hill, II, 1684
William Kendall, 1685
Arthur Allen, 1686–1688
Thomas Milner, 1691–1693
Philip Ludwell, I, 1695–1696
William Randolph, 1698
Robert Carter, 1696-1697, 1698

Sources: Cynthia Miller Leonard, comp., *The General Assembly of Virginia, July 30, 1619–January 11, 1978: A Bicentennial Register of Members* (Richmond, Va., 1978), ix; Jon Kukla, *Speakers and Clerks of the Virginia House of Burgesses, 1643–1776* (Richmond, Va., 1981).

---

* John Pory, Secretary of the Colony and a Councilor of State, styled himself "speaker" when the first General Assembly met in 1619, even though the burgesses did not sit as a house separate from the governor and Council. The Assembly remained unicameral until it divided in 1643.

** A royalist refugee who had fled Cromwell's England to escape prosecution, Smith took the alias Francis Dade.

Notes

Notes to Prologue

1. Richard Eden, *The Decades of the newe Worlde or West India* (London, 1555), Preface.

Notes to Chapter 1

1. "Letters patent to Sir Thomas Gates and others," 10 Apr. 1606, in Philip L. Barbour, ed., *The Jamestown Voyages under the First Charter, 1606–1609*, Hakluyt Society Publications, 2d Ser. (2 vols.; Cambridge, 1969), I, 31.

2. "Instructions given by way of Advice," *ca.* Nov.–Dec. 1606 in *Ibid.*, I, 34.

3. "Examination Concerning Damage to the *Susan Constant*, 13 Dec. 1606" in *Ibid.*, I, 55-56.

4. "Ode to the Virginian Voyage," in W. Reeve, ed., *The Works of Michael Drayton* (4 vols.; London, *c.a.* 1753), IV, 1367.

5. "Observations gathered out of a Discourse of the Plantation of the Southerne Colonie in Virginia by the English, 1606. Written by that Honorable Gentleman Master George Percy" in Barbour ed., *The Jamestown Voyages*, I, 133.

6. *Ibid.*

7. *Ibid.*, 134.

Notes to Chapter 2

1. Robert Beverley, *The History and Present State of Virginia*, ed. Louis B. Wright (Chapel Hill, N.C., 1947), 299, 303.

2. *Ibid.*, 303.

3. *Ibid.*, 296.

4. Peter Force, ed., *Tracts and Other Papers, Relating Principally to the Origin, Settlement, and Progress of the Colonies in North America, from the Discovery of the Country to the Year 1776* (4 vols.; Washington, D.C., 1836-1847), # XII, 20.

5. William Strachey, *Historie of Travaile into Virginia Britania* (London, 1849), 43.

6. Beverley, *History and Present State of Virginia*, 146.

7. Edward Arber and A. G. Bradley, eds., *Travels and Works of Captain John Smith, President of Virginia, and Admiral of New England, 1580-*

1631 (2 vols.; Edinburgh, 1910), I, 65.

8. *Ibid.*, I, 67.

9. *Ibid.*

Notes to Chapter 3

1. William Simmonds, *The Proceedings of the English Colonie in Virginia since their first beginning from England in the yeare of our Lord 1606, till this present 1612, with all their accidents that befell them in their Journies and Discoveries* (Oxford, 1612), 4.

2. [Gabriel Archer?], "A relatyon . . . written . . . by a gent. of the Colony," in Philip L. Barbour, ed., *The Jamestown Voyages Under the First Charter, 1606–1609*, Hakluyt Society Publications, 2d Ser. (2 vols.; Cambridge, 1969), I, 87.

3. Edward Arber and A. G. Bradley, eds., *Travels and Works of Captain John Smith, President of Virginia, and Admiral of New England, 1580–1631* (2 vols.; Edinburgh, 1910), II, 957.

4. Simmonds, *Proceedings of the English Colonie*, 4.

5. "Instructions given by way of Advice," *c.a* Nov.–Dec. 1606, in Barbour, ed., *The Jamestown Voyages*, I, 51.

6. "Observations gathered out of a Discourse of the Plantation of the Southerne Colonie in Virginia by the English, 1606. Written by that Honorable Gentleman Master George Percy," in *ibid.*, I, 142.

7. *Ibid.*, 144.

8. John Smith to the Treasurer and Council of the London Company, *c.a.* Sept.-Dec. 1608, in *ibid.*, 243.

9. Arber and Bradley, eds., *Travels and Works of Captain John Smith*, II, 446-447.

10. *Ibid.*, II, 400.

11. Simmonds, *Proceedings of the English Colonie*, 46.

12. Smith to the Treasurer, in Barbour, ed., *The Jamestown Voyages*, I, 244.

13. Newport to Robert Cecil, Earl of Salisbury, 29 July 1607, in Barbour, ed., *The Jamestown Voyages*, I, 76.

14. Arber and Bradley, eds., *Travels and Works of Captain John Smith*, II, 498.

15. *Ibid.*, II, 499.

16. Ralph Hamor, *A True Discourse of the Present Estate of Virginia, and the successe of the affaires there till the 18 of June, 1614* (London, 1615), 63.

17. *Ibid.*, 24.

18. Arber and Bradley, eds., *Travels and Works of Captain John Smith*, II, 535.

19. "A Reporte of the manner of proceeding in the General assembly convented at James citty in Virginia . . ." in Lyon G. Tyler, ed., *Narratives of Early Virginia, 1606–1625* (New York, 1907), 251.

20. *Ibid.*, 269.

21. Edward Waterhouse, "A Declaration of the state of the Colonie and Affaires in Virginia. With a Ralation of the barbarous Massacre . . ." in Susan Myra Kingsbury, ed., *Records of the Virginia Company of London* (4 vols.; Washington, D.C., 1906–1935), III, 551.

Notes to Chapter 4

1. William Waller Hening, ed. *The Statutes at Large; Being a Collection of all the Laws of Virginia, From the First Session of the Legislature in the Year 1619* (13 vols.; Richmond, New York, and Philadelphia, 1809–1823), II, 298.

2. Edmund Wingate, *An Exact Abridgment of all Statutes in Force and Use* (London, 1670), 545.

3. Sir Thomas Smith, *De Republica Anglorum, The Maner of Governement of Policie of the Realme of England . . .* (London, 1583), 33.

4. Hening, ed., *Statutes at Large*, II, 511–512.

5. Quoted in J. Frederick Fausz and Jon Kukla, eds., "A Letter of Advice to the Governor of Virginia, 1624," *William and Mary Quarterly*, 3d Ser., XXXIV (1977), 105.

6. Quoted in Warren M. Billings, ed. *The Old Dominion in the Seventeenth Century: A Documentary History of Virginia, 1606–1689* (Chapel Hill, N.C., 1975), 238.

7. H. R. McIlwaine, ed. *Journals of the House of Burgesses of Virginia, 1619-1659/60* (Richmond, Va., 1915), 27.

8. Robert Beverley, *The History and Present State of Virginia*, ed. Louis B. Wright (Chapel Hill, N.C., 1947), 240.

9. Hening, ed. *Statutes at Large*, II, 58.

10. *Ibid.*, 63.

11. Michael Dalton, *The Countrey Justice: Containing the Practice of the Justices of the Peace Out of their Sessions* (12th ed.; London, 1677), 539.

12. Beverley, *History and Present State of Virginia*, 240.

13. Henry Hartwell, James Blair, and Edward Chilton, *The Present State of Virginia and the College*, ed. Hunter Dickinson Farish (Williamsburg, Va., 1940), 34.

14. Accomack County Order Book, 1671–1673, 16 (microfilm copy, Earl K. Long Library, University of New Orleans).

15. Hening, ed., *Statutes at Large*, II, 273.

16. *Ibid.*, I, 125.

17. *Ibid.*, II, 206–207.

18. H.R. McIlwaine, ed., *Journals of the House of Burgesses of Virginia, 1659/60–1693* (Richmond, Va., 1914), 43.

19. Hartwell, Blair, and Chilton, *The Present State of Virginia*, 45.

20. James Wooley, untitled verse written in 1675 on a flyleaf of Thomas Manley, comp., *An Exact Abridgement of the Two last Volumes of Reports of Sir Edward Coke, Knight* ... (London, 1670), now in the possession of Warren M. Billings.

Notes to Chapter 5

1. John Smith, *A True Relation of such occurences and accidents of noate as hat hapned in Virginia since the first planting of that Collony* ... (London, 1608), 6.

2. De la Warr, Gates, and the Council of Virginia to Sir Thomas Smythe and the London Company, 7 July 1610 in Alexander Brown, comp., *The Genesis of the United States* (2 vols.; Boston, Mass., 1890), I, 405.

3. *Virginia Magazine of History and Biography*, XIV (1907), 381.

4. William Strachey, comp. *Lawes Divine, Morall and Martiall, etc.*, ed. David M. Flaherty (Charlottesville, Va., 1969), 19.

5. Ralph Hamor, *A True Discourse of the Present Estate of Virginia, and the successe of the affaires there till the 18 of June, 1614.* (London, 1615), 33.

6. Edward Arber and A. G. Bradley, eds., *Travels and Works of Captain John Smith, President of Virginia, and Admiral of New England, 1580–1631* (2 vols.; Edinburgh, 1910), II, 536.

7. *Ibid.*, 536.

8. "Virginia under Governor Harvey," *VMHB*, III (1895), 29.

9. William Waller Hening, ed., *The Statutes at Large; Being a Collection of all the Laws of Virginia from the First Session of the Legislature in the Year 1619* (13 vols.; Richmond, New York, and Philadelphia, 1809–1823), I, 208, 221.

10. "Virginia under Governor Harvey," *VMHB*, III (1895), 29.

11. "Instructions to Sir William Berkeley, August 1641," in Warren M. Billings, ed., *The Old Dominion in the Seventeenth Century: A Documentary History of Virginia, 1606–1689* (Chapel Hill, N.C., 1975), 54.

12. Kemp to Berkeley, 27 Feb. 1644/45, Clarendon Ms. 24, fol. 50, Bodleian Library, Oxford.

13. Peter Force, ed., *Tracts and Other Papers Relating Principally to the Origin, Settlement, and Progress of the Colonies in North America, from the Discovery of the Country to the Year 1776* (4 vols.; Washington, D.C., 1836–1847), II, #8, 3.

14. Hening, ed., *Statutes at Large*, I, 319.

15. *Ibid.*, 362.

16. *Ibid.*, II, 13.

17. *VMHB*, III (1895), 16–17.

18. Hening, ed., *Statutes at Large*, II, 172–76.

19. Ludwell to Henry Bennett, Lord Arlington, 10 Apr. 1665, Colonial Office Papers, Class 1, vol. 19, fol. 75, Public Record Office, London.

20. Berkeley to [Edward Hyde, Earl of Clarendon?], Egerton Mss. 2395, British Library, London.

Notes to Chapter 6

1. Sir William Berkeley, *A Discourse and View of Virginia* (London, 1663), 7.

2. Charles M. Andrews, ed., *Narratives of the Insurrections, 1675–1690* (New York, 1915), 16.

3. Warren M. Billings, ed., *The Old Dominion in the Seventeenth Century: A Documentary History of Virginia, 1606–1689* (Chapel Hill, N.C., 1975), 234.

4. William Waller Hening, ed., *The Statutes at Large; Being a Collection of all the Laws of Virginia from the First Session of the Legislature in the Year 1619* (13 vols.; Richmond, New York, and Philadelphia, 1809–1823), II, 332.

5. Billings, ed., *The Old Dominion in the Seventeenth Century*, 267.

6. Andrews, ed., *Narratives of the Insurrections*, 109.

7. Robert Beverley, *The History and Present State of Virginia*, ed. Louis B. Wright (Chapel Hill, N.C., 1947), 78.

8. Peter Force, ed., *Tracts and Other Papers Relating Principally to the Origin, Settlement, and Progress of the Colonies in North America, from the Discovery of the Country to the Year 1776* (4 vols.; Washington, D.C., 1836–1847), I, # XI, 28.

9. Beverley, *History and Present State of Virginia*, 78.

10. Billings, ed., *The Old Dominion in the Seventeenth Century*, 270.

11. *Ibid.*, 271.

12. *Ibid.*, 269.

13. Andrews, ed., *Narratives of the Insurrections*, 115.

14. Billings, ed., *The Old Dominion in the Seventeenth Century*, 273–274.

15. Hening, ed., *Statutes at Large*, II, 352–353, 363–364.

16. Andrews, ed., *Narratives of the Insurrections*, 116–17.

17. *Virginia Magazine of History and Biography*.

18. Andrews, *Narratives of the Insurrections*, 68, 71.

Notes to Chapter 7

1. H. R. McIlwaine, ed., *Journals of the House of Burgesses of Virginia, 1659/60–1693* (Richmond, Va., 1914), 110, 106.

2. "The Inhabitants & Freeholders to the General Assembly," Apr. 1682, Ambler Family Papers, Library of Congress, Washington, D.C.

3. Peter Force, ed., *Tracts and Other Papers Relating Principally to the Origin, Settlement, and Progress of the Colonies in North America, from*

the Discovery of the Country to the Year 1776 (4 vols.; Washington, D.C., 1836–1847), III, # XII, 24.

4. McIlwaine, ed., *JHB, 1659/60–1693*, 174, 226, 257.

5. *Ibid.*, 245.

6. Colonial Office Papers, Class 5, vol. 1371, p. 63, Public Record Office, London.

7. Culpeper to Judith Culpeper, 14 May 1680, Culpeper Family Papers, Kent Archives Office, Maidstone, Kent.

8. *Virginia Magazine of History and Biography*, XIV (1907), 364.

Notes to Chapter 8

1. Hugh Jones, *The Present State of Virginia . . .* , ed. Richard L. Morton (1724; Chapel Hill, N.C., 1956), 25.

2. *Ibid.*

3. John Scott Rawlings, *Virginia's Colonial Churches: An Architectural Guide* (Richmond, Va., 1963), 24.

4. Quoted in the *Weekly Williamsburg Gazette*, 20 May 1857.

5. Alonzo T. Dill *et al.*, *The 350th Anniversary of Jamestown, 1607–1957: Final Report to the President and Congress of the Jamestown–Williamsburg–Yorktown Celebration Commission* (Washington, D.C., 1958), 20, 58.

Suggested Readings

[*While all of the following titles can be found in a college, university, or historical society library, most are generally available in public libraries as well. — * Available in paperback.*]

Charles M. Andrews, ed. *Narratives of the Insurrections, 1675-1690.* New York, 1915.

Edward Arber and A. G. Bradley, eds. *The Travels and Works of Captain John Smith.* Edinburgh, 1910.

Philip L. Barbour, ed. *The Jamestown Voyages under the First Charter, 1606-1609.* Hakluyt Society Publications, 2d Ser., CXXXVI-CXXXVII. Cambridge, 1969.

Samuel M. Bemiss, ed. *The Three Charters of the Virginia Company of London, with Seven Related Documents, 1606-1621.* Williamsburg, Va., 1957.

* Warren M. Billings, ed. *The Old Dominion in the Seventeenth Century: A Documentary History of Virginia, 1606-1689.* Chapel Hill, N.C., 1975.

_____. "The Transfer of English Law to Virginia, 1606-1650," in *The Westward Enterprise: English Activities in Ireland, the Atlantic, and America, 1480-1650,* ed. K. R. Andrews, N. P. Canny, and P.E.H. Hair. Liverpool, 1978.

_____. *Their Majesties' Governor and Captain-General of Virginia.* Fairfax, Va., 1990.

Warren M. Billings, John E. Selby, and Thad W. Tate. *Colonial Virginia — A History.* White Plains, N.Y., 1986.

Philip Alexander Bruce. *Economic History of Virginia in the Seventeenth Century.* New York, 1895.

_____. *Institutional History of Virginia in the Seventeenth Century.* New York, 1910.

* John L. Cotter and J. Paul Hudson. *New Discoveries at Jamestown: Site of the First Successful English Settlement in America.* Washington, D.C., 1957.

Wesley Frank Craven. *The Dissolution of the Virginia Company: The Failure of a Colonial Experiment.* New York, 1932.

* _____. *White, Red, and Black: The Seventeenth-Century Virginian.* Charlottesville, Va., 1971.

Richard Hakluyt, *The Principall Navigations Voiages and Discoveries of the English Nation: A Facsimile Edition of 1589, with an Introduction by D.B. Quinn and R.A. Shelton and with a New Index by Alison Quinn*. Hakluyt Society Publications, Extra Ser., XXXIX. Cambridge, 1965.

* Francis P. Jennings. *The Invasion of America: Indians, Colonialism, and the Cant of Conquest*. Chapel Hill, N.C., 1975.

Susan Myra Kingsbury, ed. *The Records of the Virginia Company of London*. Washington, D.C., 1906–1935.

* Edmund S. Morgan. *American Slavery, American Freedom: The Ordeal of Colonial Virginia*. New York, 1975.

David Beers Quinn. *England and the Discovery of America, 1481–1620*. New York, 1973.

* A. L Rowse. *The England of Elizabeth*. New York, 1951.

* William Strachey, comp. *For the Colony of Virginea Britannia: Lawes Divine, Morall and Martiall, etc.*, ed. David H. Flaherty. Charlottesville, Va., 1969.

Lyon G. Tyler, ed. *Narratives of Early Virginia, 1607–1625*. New York, 1907.

William L. Shea. *The Virginia Militia in the Seventeenth Century*. Baton Rouge, La., 1983.

* Thad W. Tate and David L. Ammerman. *The Chesapeake in the Seventeenth Century: Essays in Anglo-American Society*. Chapel Hill, N.C., 1979.

* Alden T. Vaughan. *American Genesis: Captain John Smith and the Founding of Virginia*. Boston, Mass., 1975.

J. Leitch Wright, Jr. *The Only Land They Knew: The Tragic Story of the American Indians in the Old South*. New York, 1981.

Illustration Credits

Association for the Preservation of Virginia Antiquities - p. 106

A Brief and True Report of the New Found Land of Virginia by Thomas Harriot (Dover Publications, New York, 1972) - pp. 23, 25, 26 & 27

Colonial National Historical Park - pp. 11, 14, 17, 36, 37, 38, 40, 48, 50, 52 (bottom), 56, 77, 97, 107, 108, 111, 114, 115, 116, 117 & 119

Sidney E. King painting, courtesy of Colonial NHP - pp. 16, 18, 32, 39, 44, 46, 49, 52 (top), 70, 75, 78, 87, 94 & 104

Dean S. Thomas - pp. 19, 21 & 53

Virginia Portraiture (Virginia Historical Society, Richmond) - pp. 12, 13, 34, 43, 59 & 80

About the Author

Warren M. Billings is a Virginian who once lived at Jamestown. A specialist in the study of seventeenth-century Virginia as well as the fields of early American and legal history, he is the author of six books and numerous articles for scholarly journals. He is Professor of History at the University of New Orleans and Historian of the Supreme Court of Louisiana.